GEORGIA PLACE-NAMES
from JOT-EM-DOWN to DOCTORTOWN

CATHY J. KAEMMERLEN

THE
History
PRESS

Published by The History Press
Charleston, SC
www.historypress.com

Front cover, top row, left: photo by Robert Gaare; *center*: photo by Robert Gaare; *right*: photo by Robert Gaare; *middle row, left*: photo by Ren Davis; *center*: photo by Robert Gaare; *right*: photo by Robert Gaare; *bottom row, left*: Library of Congress; *center*: photo by Robert Gaare; *right*: stock photo.
Back cover: photo by Cathy Kaemmerlen, taken at the Bartow Museum.

First published 2019

Manufactured in the United States

ISBN 9781467143554

Library of Congress Control Number: 2019937045

Notice: The information in this book is true and complete to the best of our knowledge. It is offered without guarantee on the part of the author or The History Press. The author and The History Press disclaim all liability in connection with the use of this book.

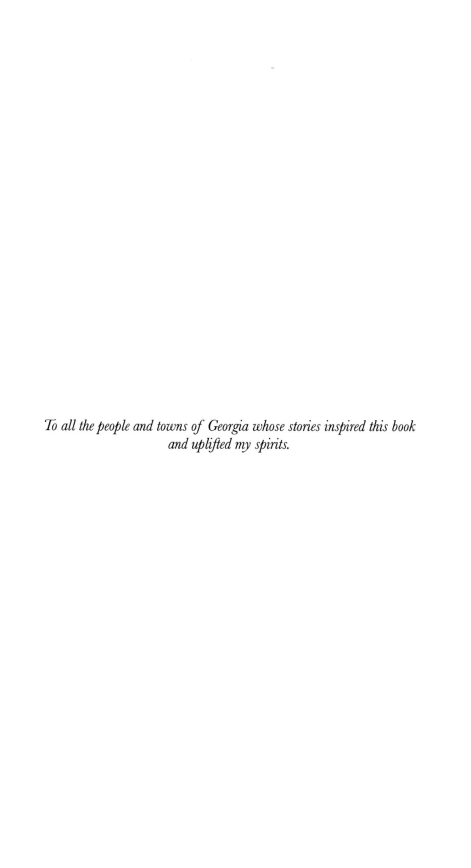

To all the people and towns of Georgia whose stories inspired this book and uplifted my spirits.

CONTENTS

CONTENTS

Contents

RESOURCES

There are many resources I used in compiling information for this Georgia place-name book. My journey started with Kenneth Krakow's *Georgia's Place-Names: Their History and Origins*, now in its third edition thanks to the work of his children. *Placenames of Georgia: Essays of John H. Goff* edited by Francis Lee Utley and Marion R. Hemperley; *How Georgia Got Her Names* by Hal E. Brinkley; *Cyclopedia of Georgia* by Allen D. Candler and Clement A. Evans; *Georgia, A Guide to Its Towns*; and *The New Georgia Guide* by Steve Owen and Jane Posers Weldon were invaluable in helping me collect the names of towns that interested me and some of their origins. I also found these books very helpful: *Georgia: Comprising Sketches of Counties, Towns, Events, Institutions, and Persons* by Allen Daniel Candler; *Atlanta and Environs* by Franklin Garrett; *Georgia's Landmarks, Memorials and Legends in 2 Volumes* by Lucian Lamar Knight; *Georgia, A Guide to Its Towns and Countryside*, under the auspices of the WPA/Federal Writers' Project; *American Guide Series/Georgia*, in conjunction with the Georgia Board of Education; and *Georgia Curiosities* by William Schemmel. All of these books were located in the Georgia Room of my county's main library.

The following interesting books gave me information on certain areas of the state: *Georgia's Land of the Golden Isles* by Burnett Vanstory; *God, Dr. Buzzards and the Bolito Man* by Cornelia Walker Bailey; and *Rock City Barns* by David B. Jenkins. Georgia Public Broadcasting's *Hometown USA* series was fun to watch and brought to visual life what I had been reading about. Fun to look at on the internet was the site Really Weird Place Names (reallyweirdplacenames.blogspot.com). Past issues of *Georgia Backroads Magazine* were very helpful for background stories, as were issues of *GEMC Georgia Magazine* (www.georgiamagazine.org).

Some information was acquired through questions submitted to town chambers of commerce or historical societies, as well as visits to various places to obtain information firsthand. Some of these places were the Museum at Tunnel Hill, Barrow County Historical Society, Jerusalem Lutheran Church, Claxton Fruitcake Bakery, Santa Claus and Bethlehem, the Sautee-Nacoochee Folk Pottery Museum, the Rabbittown Café, the Martin Lutheran King Memorial site in Dublin, the Bigfoot Museum in Cherry Log, the Cherry Log Fall Festival, the Vidalia Onion Museum, Myrtle Hill Cemetery and others. Talking to people who know and love their town was most beneficial.

In truth, the most valuable resources were the publications of various county historical societies. I won't name them all, as Georgia has 159 counties, and I looked at every possible publication. But there are a few that are outstanding, namely: *Sketches of Bartow County* compiled by J.B. Tate; *Bartow County Georgia Heritage Book, Volume 1*; *Wayfarers in Walton* by Anita B. Sams; and *The History of DeKalb County, Georgia 1822–1900* by Vivian Saffold Price.

Please note that, in all chapters, place-names appear in **bold**, followed by the county in parenthesis. Towns mentioned only briefly, as former towns, appear in *italics*.

ACKNOWLEDGEMENTS

I could not have written this book without the help of so many people who spoke up with suggestions of towns, or knowledge of towns, or connections with towns. I have tried to remember and acknowledge them all and hope I am not leaving anyone out.

Thanks to the staff at the Georgia Room at the Switzer Public Library in Marietta, Georgia. The collection there is quite wonderful, and the staff were very helpful in directing me to the right locations and in reshelving the massive, heavy books I accumulated by the end of each visit.

Thanks to Tom Krakow, son of Ken Krakow, author of *Georgia's Place-Names*, or, as I called it, the Bible, for his approval of my project. Thanks to dear friend Betty Ann Wylie and her old friend Ann Harris, the Nancy Drews of Americus, Georgia. Also in Americus, thanks to Gary Fisk for information about the Merry Cusses and homebrewers. Special thanks to Al Stephens, Jan Galt, Vivian Saffold Price, Gary Greene and Mary Elena Kirk for their interest and all-consuming knowledge of their towns.

Ren Davis, photographer, historian and author, was most generous in providing a photograph of Jasper Newton Smith. Cynthia Jennings also contributed a photo. Bobbie Seabert at the Folk Pottery Museum in Sautee-Nachoochee, Cheekea Cromer at the Barrow County Museum and Malinda Bakara of the Bigfoot Museum in Cherry Log were among the many wonderful tour guides who answered my many questions.

The following people contributed names of towns they thought would be of interest—proof to me that this book might actually have an audience:

Kelly Jackson, Mary Price, Judy Longsworth, Clara Cobb, Ron Anglin, Amy Reed, Mary Hamilton, Lisa Russell and her son and Fran Jeskey Bollinger.

Special thanks to my commissioning editor at The History Press, Joe Garnell, for his support, encouragement and patience about my "lackings" in the world of technology.

And last but not least, thanks to my husband, Robert Gaare, for accompanying me on these trips to places far and wide, helping me to gather the stories and information for the book and for having patience with my exuberance over a sought-after and found place or landmark. He was the official photographer for the book and sometimes tromped through mud and back roads in order to get the right shot.

INTRODUCTION

As a storyteller and a thirty-year Georgia resident, I have long been fascinated with collecting stories that help me to know the people, legends, festivals, events, folklore, products, symbols and history of my state. There is an endless abundance of material proving Georgians love where they live, love their communities and relish their town histories. I am honored to pass on these stories and tell them as authentically and as accurately as possible.

In traveling the state, visiting the wonders that each town possesses, I have found a new respect and love for my state and the people who dwell here. Each community offers something of interest. Each community has a story or two or three to tell. Each town has historians, thank goodness, who keep the records alive from the past and present.

In trying to decide what my book should be about, I became fascinated with strange names I encountered, like Ty Ty and Doctortown and Po'Biddy Crossroads and Jot-Em-Down. How did the residents of these towns come up with these names? What's the derivation? How many names did the town go through before it settled on its current name? Was there an Indian influence? Who was the town named for? Is there an interesting story behind the name?

I drew some obvious conclusions. First, Indian influences are everywhere in Georgia. There was no way I could mention or research them all. Second, many towns were named for generals or railroad engineers or postmasters, etc. There was no way I could mention all of these men. Towns named for women, however—wives, sisters and daughters—are fewer and farther between. So, I devoted a chapter to towns named for women. Third, many towns are named for cities in other lands, like Berlin, Bremen and Buena Vista. Again, there are far too many to mention, so I chose the ones that had the most interesting stories to tell. Fourth, there are many, many towns named for flowers, fruit, Georgia products and animals. I picked and chose among an assortment of these. Fifth, there are the spas and springs, and towns named for them—again, far too numerous, so, again, I made some selective choices.

There are several Georgia place-name books that attempt to be all-inclusive or encyclopedic. This is not that kind of book, although I mention over two hundred towns. I have really just scratched the surface in regard to place-names. And I haven't even tried to include streets, rivers, creeks, valleys and mountains, which would make the book even more inclusive in terms of names of all kinds of places in the state.

I picked and chose among the many and tried to include a wide range from all parts of the state. Naturally, I was drawn to the unusual, the humorous, the ironic, even the tragic. I learned what a po'mouth name is—and there are plenty of those names—representing in-jokes among early settlers and pioneers, such as Hardup and Buttermilk Bottoms. I loved learning about the coined names, such as Subligna and Redan. I loved learning about the whimsical names, like Hopeulikit, Deepstep and Hahira.

I learned that almost every town has at least two explanations for the origin of the name. One is always the historical one, named after someone or something of value. The other and more interesting one is the folklore version. I'm guessing that the folklore version is the one that will stick with the reader. Again, as a storyteller, I love the folklore versions because they make the town more endearing. Stories bind us together. I tried to hit upon as many stories as I could find, but again, it would take years of research and a massive missal to be all-inclusive.

Researching this book took me on a whirlwind tour of Georgia history, from Oglethorpe to the Revolutionary War, the Trail of Tears, the Civil War, the Industrial Revolution and more. I am convinced that history is all about the stories that come from the people who lived through these times and wrote about them. I felt as if I were traveling through time. And I felt enlightened and encouraged by the bravery, courage, humor, humanity and creativity of the people of Georgia. People love to share their stories, and I was so lucky to hear them—at least enough to fill this book and more!

I found it wasn't enough just to tell the origin stories of the towns. What made the towns really come to life were the unique features and festivals and legends. How can you mention Tunnel Hill without telling the story of the Great Locomotive Chase, or mention Cherry Log without talking about the Bigfoot Museum, or mention Sautee-Nacoochee without telling the love story of Sautee and Nacoochee?

This book turned into a travelogue of sorts, with tangential features about interesting sites to see all over the state. How could I not include the story of Hogzilla in Hahira? (I am a believer.) Or the story of taxidermist Bud Jones of Tallapoosa, whose stuffed possum is dropped every New Year's Eve? Or the story of Joe Rogers and Tom Forkner, who came up with the idea of creating a twenty-four-hour, seven-day-a-week fast-food restaurant called Waffle House in Avondale Estates? Or the story of Xavier Roberts, who created Cabbage Patch Dolls and the Cabbage Patch Hospital in Cleveland, Georgia? And there are so many more stories that I just had to tell.

It is my hope to take you along with me as I recount the adventures I experienced while writing this book. I hope you will find the stories enlightening, informative and smile-producing. And I hope you will be encouraged to explore Georgia from mountains to the Piedmont to the coast. Enjoy!

THE PLACE-NAME STORIES

1

SOUNDS LIKE GREEK, ROMAN, FRENCH, GERMAN AND IRISH TO ME

There are a number of Georgia towns named after cities around the world, but only European cities are mentioned in this chapter. We'll start with a trip to Greece—actually, Georgia's version of it—and a tribute to the publisher of this book, Arcadia Publishing / The History Press.

The mission of Arcadia Press is "to showcase America's unique history through the places and people that have helped to create it." But why choose the name *Arcadia*? And what does *Arcadia* mean? It is the feminine version of the Greek word *Arcas*, meaning a region offering peace and contentment in an unspoiled paradise. Through Arcadia's publications, books can certainly sweep us away into different worlds, times and characters.

Arcadia (Liberty—the name of the county Arcadia is in) was also named for that idyllic joy found in Peloponnese, Greece, where Sparta, Corinth and Argos were located. Its pastoral people, in spite of a recurring history of being conquered and reconquered, lived in harmony in a rustic setting close to nature. Arcadia was the home of Pan and his court of fairies, who created an idealized version of paradise.

Staying with Greek influences, a phoenix is a mythological bird that rises from the ashes, symbolizing a hopeful future. This was certainly the case for **Phoenix** (Putnam), a town that was rebuilt after Indians burned down the early settlement. Another Georgia phoenix city is Atlanta, often referred to as the "Phoenix City," which rose from the ashes of the Civil War.

A painting depicting the idyllic, pastoral life in Arcadia of ancient Greece. *Library of Congress*.

Alexander H. Stephens, vice-president of the Confederacy and a Georgia native, was asked to suggest a name for a new town in Oglethorpe County. He chose **Philomath** (pronounced "Fye-low-math), which is Greek for "love of knowledge." His friend and distant cousin, John W. Reid, started a prominent boys' academy there.

When in Rome, do as the Romans do. **Rome**, Georgia (Floyd), received its Italian name, as the story goes, when five travelers met by a spring and agreed to found a city. The name would be drawn from a hat. Colonel Daniel R. Mitchell wrote "Rome" on a slip of paper, as the city's landscape reminded him of Rome, Italy. His slip was chosen.

There is a statue in front of the Municipal Auditorium in Rome, Georgia, of the Capitoline Wolf, a mythical she-wolf, suckling the twins Romulus and Remus, whose mythological story recalls the events that led to the founding of the city of Rome and the Roman Kingdom of Romulus.

The twins were descended from Greek and Latin nobility. King Amulius saw them as a possible threat to his rule, so he ordered them killed. Abandoned on the banks of the Tiber River, they were saved by Tiberinus, the god of the river, and survived with the care of others, supposedly suckled by a she-wolf and then adopted by a shepherd. This area would eventually become Rome.

Romulus and Remus statue in front of the Rome Municipal Auditorium. *Photo by Robert Gaare.*

As a young adult, Remus was kidnapped after his true identity was revealed. Would Remus attempt to overthrow the king? What would his twin brother do? Romulus and his band rescued Remus and had their grandfather rightfully restored to the throne. Later on, the two disagreed vehemently over which of the Seven Hills should be used to build the capital city. Remus was killed by Romulus, or one of his supporters, in a power coup. Romulus then went on to found the city of Rome and reigned there for many years as its first king.

As a gift, Benito Mussolini sent a replica of the original statue to its sister city in Georgia with the inscription, "This statue of the Capitoline Wolf—as a forecast of prosperity and glory—has been sent from ancient Rome to new Rome during the consulship of Benito Mussolini in the year 1929."

We all know what happened to the consulship of Benito Mussolini. Rome, Georgia, has fared much better, except for the kidnapping of one of the twins (meaning the statues of Romulus and Remus) in 1933. Was this a

Tombstone of First Lady Ellen Axson Wilson at the Myrtle Hill Cemetery. *Photo by Robert Gaare.*

copycat act from the story of the founding of Rome or just a coincidental act of vandalism? Neither the twin nor the kidnapper was ever found. Another twin was sent from Italy to replace the missing one. Italy became one of our Axis enemies during World War II. For safekeeping, the statue was put in storage because of the many threats to dynamite and destroy it during wartime.

Mrs. Woodrow Wilson, Ellen Axson Wilson, standing by some of her paintings. *Library of Congress.*

Like Rome, Italy, the town of Rome, Georgia, is known as the city of the Seven Hills and Three Rivers. It is also the birthplace of Ellen Axson Wilson, First Lady and wife of Woodrow Wilson, and her burial place in Rome's Myrtle Hill Cemetery. She was invited to attend a 1914 homecoming event in Rome, as its most impressive former resident, but she died two months earlier at the White House of Bright's disease. She arrived in a coffin instead of a carriage.

Monument to the Women of the Civil War at Myrtle Hill Cemetery. *Photo by Robert Gaare.*

Myrtle Hill Cemetery also boasts a poignant statue of the women of the Confederacy, the first to be erected to honor the role of women in the Civil War. It was erected by President Theodore Roosevelt in 1910 with an inscription by Woodrow Wilson.

> *To the women of the Confederacy*
> *whose purity, fidelity, whose courage, whose gentle genius*
> *in love and counsels kept the home secure…*
> *In peace a time of healing,*
> *the guardians of our tranquility and of our strength.*

Avondale Estates (DeKalb) is a planned village, modeled after Shakespeare's birthplace, *Stratford-upon-Avon*. In the 1890s, lots were sold in the area. George Francis Willis, a patent-medicine magnate, purchased the entire village in 1928 to create a Tudor-style community with the feel of an English village. It is listed in the National Register of Historic Places and

Frontage shot of Avondale Estates, modeled after Shakespeare's England. *Photo by Robert Gaare.*

boasts the location of the first Waffle House, which opened its doors on Labor Day weekend, 1955.

Joe Rogers and Tom Forkner had an idea to start a business they could own. Their idea was to start a restaurant focused on people and serving quality food at a great value. The first Waffle House opened in Avondale Estates, and a legend was born. Now the "yellow signed" icon looms over 2,100 restaurants in twenty-five states, and the chain expands yearly. Each employee is trained to greet customers with a heartfelt "Hello," keeping the original promise to focus on people.

It is said that if you added all the cups of coffee that Waffle Houses pour each year, it would be enough to fill nearly eight Olympic-sized swimming pools. If you stacked all of the sausage patties that Waffle Houses serve in a year on top of each other, the pile would be nearly four times the height of the Empire State Building. If you laid end to end all of the Smithfield Bacon that Waffle Houses serve in a year, it would wrap all the way around the equator. Open twenty-four hours a day, 365 days a year, serving breakfast foods and more, the restaurant has a saying: "Waffle House doors have no locks."

German Village (Glynn), on the extreme southeast end of St. Simon's Island, was settled by the Salzburgers, who came to Georgia with James Oglethorpe. They were to make wares and grow food to provide for the soldiers at Fort Frederica. They named it German Village. When Oglethorpe's regiment disbanded in 1749, the Salzburgers left St. Simon's Island. (More on this story appears in chapter 11, under **Ebenezer.**)

Helen (White) is the new Alpine German village in Georgia. It is the third most-visited city in Georgia, next to Atlanta and Savannah. (There is more to read about Helen in chapter 3.)

Ooh la la. Here comes the French influence, starting with **La Grange** (Troup), the city that takes its name from General Marquis de Lafayette's estate in France. Lafayette was the French soldier and statesman who earned recognition as a supporter of, and fighter for, American independence from England during the Revolutionary War. Said to be the son that George Washington never had, Lafayette came to visit La Grange in 1825 and remarked that the area reminded him of his home in France, the Villa La Grange.

Fortunately, the town was spared burning during the Civil War, thanks to the Nancy Harts, the only women's militia recognized by the Confederacy. Less than one hundred in number, they bravely lined up with their antiquated guns to face several thousand Yankees. General William

Original Waffle House, located in Avondale Estates. *Photo by Robert Gaare.*

Author flipping hash browns at the original Waffle House in Avondale Estates. *Photo by Robert Gaare.*

T. Sherman's Union troops were impressed by the women's bravery, describing them as "dressed in heterogeneous costumes." In a show of gratitude for saving their town, the Nancy Harts cooked the Yankee invaders a homemade chicken dinner. The Nancy Harts were named after the Georgia Revolutionary War heroine (whose story is briefly told in chapter 17 under **Hornet's Nest.**)

Louisville (Jefferson), pronounced "Lewis-ville," was Georgia's third capital, from 1795 to 1806. The town was laid out and patterned after the city of Philadelphia but named to honor Louis XVI of France in appreciation for French aid during the American Revolution. It is home to one of the few standing slave markets in the South. Hanging in the market is a bell sent in 1772 by the king of France as a gift to a convent in New Orleans. The bell was captured by pirates, sold in Savannah and later sent to the new capital of Georgia, Louisville.

Louisville is also the site of the burning of the infamous Yazoo fraud papers. Speculative land companies bought thirty-five million acres of Georgia, Alabama and Mississippi land near the Yazoo River for less than one and a half cents an acre. There was a statewide wave of indignation, causing the legislature to pass an act rescinding the sale. All records of the transaction were destroyed. A mysterious "white haired stranger" used a sunglass to start the fires at the Louisville Courthouse. Later, the U.S. Supreme Court declared this act of the Georgia legislature unconstitutional. A landmark decision, *Fletcher v. Peck*, marked one of the first times the Supreme Court overturned a state law, citing that the land sales were binding contracts and could not be retroactively invalidated. The issue was finally resolved in an 1814 settlement with the claimants.

There is also a city named **Lafayette** (Walker) named to honor the Marquis de Lafayette.

This brings us to the Irish contingency in Georgia. In **Dublin** (Laurens), an Irishman named Jonathan Sawyer, who had a sawmill, agreed to donate land for the public buildings of the town, provided it be named for Erin's (the Emerald Isle of Ireland) capital. It was said he did this to please his wife, who was originally from Dublin, Ireland. (In James Joyce's book *Finnegans Wake*, he mentions Laurens County and Jonathan Sawyer in this excerpt: "Topsawyer's rocks by the stream Oconee exaggerated themselse to Laurens County's gorgios while they went doublin their mumper all the time.")

A surprise and a little-known treat of Dublin is that fifteen-year-old Martin Luther King, a student at Booker T. Washington High School in

Downtown Dublin memorial to Martin Luther King, where he gave his first speech at the African Baptist Church. *Photo by Robert Gaare.*

Atlanta, delivered his first speech, titled "The Negro and the Constitution," on April 17, 1944, in Dublin. The Colored Elk Clubs of Georgia held their state convention at the First African Baptist Church in the Irish-named town and sponsored a statewide essay contest. King entered and ended his speech with these words, "My heart throbs anew in the hope that inspired by the example of Lincoln, imbued with the spirit of Christ, they will cast down the last barrier to perfect freedom. And I, with my brother of blackest hues possessing at last my rightful heritage and holding my head erect may stand beside the Saxon—a Negro—and yet a man!" Little did the audience know what they were witnessing, who was speaking and that this was to be the first speech of many in Dr. King's twenty-five-year struggle for civil rights for African Americans.

The site of his speech is now a memorial park, next to the First African Church. You can listen to an audiotape of his transcribed speech as well as the story of his struggles. There is a seven-foot-high sculpture by Corey Barksdale capturing the theme of the memorial park—"Sound waves that

Statue honoring Martin Luther King by Corey Barksdale in front of the African Baptist Church in Dublin. *Photo by Robert Gaare.*

sent shock waves around the world"—and a ten-foot-high by fifty-four-foot-wide mural, also by Barksdale, depicting a young girl's wish for a better tomorrow and the need for future generations to carry on Dr. King's legacy of peace, love and unity.

On the bus ride home to Atlanta, King was asked for the first time in his life to give up his seat and stand at the back of the bus. His first inclination was to refuse, but his teacher convinced him to do otherwise. Rosa Parks and others soon followed suit and did the real refusing.

The Atlanta Rolling Mill was destroyed after the Battle of Atlanta in the Civil War. On its site, the Fulton Bag and Cotton Mill, owned by Jacob Elsas, began its operations in 1881. **Cabbagetown** (Fulton) became the mill town surrounding the operation, whose primary product was cotton bags for packaging agricultural products. In search of cheap labor, Elsas recruited poor whites from the Appalachian region of north Georgia, many of them Scotch-Irish immigrants. He built a small community of one- and two-story shotgun houses and cottages for the mill workers. He also provided

Mural painted on the stone wall at the entrance to Cabbagetown. *Photo by Robert Gaare.*

his workers with security, medical and dental services, a library, a nursery, even an occasional picture show. In this tightly knit community, all lives were connected to the mill in every way. The community was first known as Fulton Mill Village. But how did it get to be known as Cabbagetown? There are several stories.

These Scotch-Irish mill workers supposedly grew cabbages in their front yards. The odor of cabbage cooking is very distinct, so the area began to be called Cabbagetown.

Another story says that at one of the main intersections of the narrow roads that made up Cabbagetown, a Ford Model T flipped over and spilled its cargo of cabbages on the street. Not wanting to hunt for all the rolling cabbages, the driver purportedly shouted, "Free cabbages for all!" The smell of cabbage cooking all day filled the community. It became a cabbagetown. Some versions have a train, not the Model T, full of cabbages derailing and spilling its load.

Still another story was told by Marion "Peanut" Brown, who moved to Cabbagetown in 1919 and got her first job peddling produce on foot, carrying her baskets of sweet potatoes door to door. She met Joe Newman, who had a mule-drawn wagon. They began peddling together, Fridays and Saturdays being their best days. They found that cabbages sold better than anything else, so they decided to take entire loads of nothing but cabbages into town. This was the beginning of the name Cabbagetown.

In the end, everyone seems to have their own version of how Cabbagetown came to be named.

The mill closed in 1977, one year after being named to the National Register of Historic Places. The surrounding neighborhoods began to decline, until the yuppies and millennials took over. Now a hip place to live, the former Cotton Mill has been turned into lofts. A small setback occurred in 2008, when a tornado ripped through the area. After the cleanup, mill houses began to be renovated, with the addition of second-story pop-ups. Young families find Cabbagetown a desirable place to live.

The Krog Street Tunnel connecting Cabbagetown to Inman Park is covered with interesting, ever-changing graffiti. The tunnel leads to the very popular Krog Street Indoor Market and the start of Atlanta's Beltline, a walking, jogging and biking trail lined with shops and restaurants and featuring delicious smells coming up and down the trail. And I don't mean cabbage-cooking smells!

There is a historic Cabbagetown in Toronto, Canada, with a similar history. Irish immigrants fled the potato famine, settled in Toronto and grew

The author's daughter, Sara Brune, holding a recently extracted Cabbage Patch Doll at the Cleveland Baby General Hospital. *Photo by Robert Gaare.*

cabbages in their front yard. It became "the worst Anglo Saxon slum in North America" but is now one of Toronto's most gentrified neighborhoods.

We have to take a side trip to **Cleveland**, Georgia (White), home of the Cabbage Patch Kids and Babyland General Hospital. It all started in 1978 with Xavier Roberts, who had a brainstorm that homely, handsewn cloth dolls with soft, sculptured faces, using a needle molding technique, could be sold for exorbitant prices. And they were. In 1983, the dolls became mass produced with plastic faces and were sold for more reasonable prices. There was a great demand for the dolls. Many a mother and grandmother scratched and clawed their way to grab that last Cabbage Patch Doll on the shelf, satisfying a daughter or granddaughter who said she'd die without getting one for Christmas. Over 115 million have been sold, with many people becoming collectors and owning hundreds of the various kinds of Cabbage Patch Dolls that have been issued.

Roberts had another brainstorm—to create a hospital for tourists and fans to see where the dolls are birthed (of course, in a cabbage patch). He purchased a seventy-thousand-square-foot building in time to celebrate the twenty-fifth anniversary of the dolls. Several times a day, visitors can witness a new doll emerging from a head of cabbage. It's the birthing chamber! An LPN (Licensed Patch Nurse) calls out "Code Green!," and the birthing process begins, with narration about dilating leaves, stem pressure and chlorophyll counts before she yanks out a new baby, turns it upside-down, spanks its bottom and swaddles it in a blanket. Some lucky child gets to name the new baby, and an even luckier child gets to buy it and adopt it for a pretty big chunk of green, for this is one of those original cloth-faced dolls, the expensive kind.

Each child who ends up purchasing a doll from the pretty overwhelming selection in the gift shop goes to an adoption center, where the specialist in the room helps them name the doll. Then the specialist conducts a ceremony. The child must promise to cherish the doll forever and ever, while parents ooh and aah and take videos and pictures for the child's scrapbook. Of course, you have to buy a doll bed. And doll clothes for every occasion…and pets for the doll…and the list goes on and on. You will leave with a shortage of "greens" in your pocketbook.

2

LOCATION, LOCATION, LOCATION

Any real estate agent will tell you that location is the single most important aspect when considering investing in a piece of property. The locations of the towns noted in this chapter were the deciding factor in determining their names. There are too many to list, but here are a few key ones.

Center Point (Caroll) is named for its approximately equal distance from *Carrollton* and *Villa Rica*.

Centerville (Houston) was so named because it is centered between *Byron* and *Warner Robins* to the east–west and *Macon* and *Perry* to the north–south. There was an earlier settlement called **Centerville**, **Center Village** or **Centre Village** (Charlton) that was named because it was a central trading village in the early 1800s, located on the St. Mary's River.

Great caravans of farmers came in the fall and winter months and brought their wares to sell. There's a story of a man from nearby Coffee County who brought a horse cart of chickens. When he found no market for his hens, he found solace by imbibing rather freely at the local saloons. Whiskey sold for $1.25 a gallon and New England rum for $1.00 a gallon. Going back to his cart, he decided to liberate the chickens. He swore he would neither haul them back nor give them away, so he turned them loose to fend for themselves. It is said that those chickens and their descendants roamed the streets of Center Village for years.

The town was a metropolitan center but also a meeting place for settling disputes. Some ended in macho displays. Fistfights, mostly fair, with only a few killings, was the usual way to settle the boast of who was best or right.

Also prevalent in these center villages was horse racing and other sports, attracting various dandies and sportsmen.

The town declined after the Civil War, when the railroads decided to bypass the town. No one knows what became of the chickens.

A-Yeh-li-a-lo-Hee (Hart) is the Cherokee name for **Center of the World**. It was a Cherokee Assembly Ground. Cherokee trails radiated in all directions from this hub. Cherokees gathered here to hold their councils, to dance and worship and to barter their hides, furs and blankets with the white traders who came from Augusta.

The Center of the World was also a noted roost for passenger pigeons. It was said at one time that the passenger pigeons were so great in number that their combined weight broke the tree limbs where they roosted. We know what happened to the passenger pigeons. They are extinct. And the Cherokees, in a way, became extinct in the area, too, when they were driven out by the Treaty of New Echota. The treaty was signed by some Cherokee leaders, who were later killed by fellow tribesmen for being traitors to the Cherokee Nation. Andrew Jackson was president at the time.

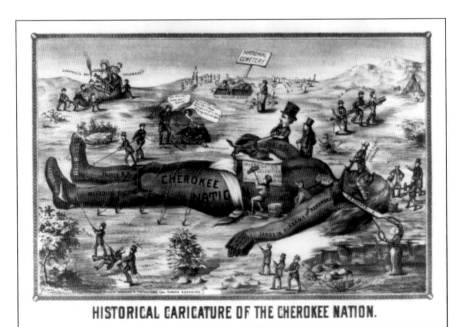

HISTORICAL CARICATURE OF THE CHEROKEE NATION.

Cartoon depicting the fate of the Cherokee Indians in Georgia. *Library of Congress.*

The name "Center of the World" stayed, and the town was now used by the white settlers as a rendezvous point for hunting parties for years to come.

The town is no more, like the passenger pigeons and the Cherokees. There once was a gift shop where you could buy Center of the World T-shirts. No more. There is another Center of the World located in California. Buy your T-shirts there.

Towns were often named because of their proximity to railway junctions or crossroads. For example, **Junction City** (Talbot), as the name implies, was the site of several railroad junctions. **Waycross** (Ware) was named by early settlers because many roads crossed here. **Union City** (Fulton) was named for the meeting of two railroads: the Atlanta and West Point Line and the Seaboard Coast Line.

Alto (Habersham) is a coined name for Altus, meaning the high point of the railroad line, similar to **Zenith** (Crawford) being the highest point of the railroad line between Columbus and Macon. **Climax** (Decatur) is named for its "lofty" elevation, being the highest point of the railroad between Savannah and the Chattahoochee River.

The climax of the year in Climax, Georgia, appears to be the Swine Time Festival, held the first Saturday after Thanksgiving. More than thirty-five thousand visitors arrive to see who wins these contests: hog calling, best dressed pig, pig racing, baby crawling, chitterlings eating, corn shucking and the crowning of Miss and Little Miss Swine Time.

Six Miles (Floyd), first known as Courtesy, was so named for being the rail post six miles from Rome, Georgia.

Omega (Tift and Colquitt) acquired its name because it was the last rail stop going southward in Georgia. Omega is the last letter of the Greek alphabet. **Relay** (Floyd) was a rest stop or place to change a team of horses on the old stagecoach road from Rome to Cedartown. **Stonesthrow** (Hall), now known as *Gillsville*, was a stone's throw from Maysville.

The name **Willacoochee** (Atkinson) doesn't represent the fact that it is one half mile each way from the Brunswick and Western Railways. Its name comes from a Native American word meaning either "little river" or "home of the wildcat."

Midville (Burke) was so named because it is halfway between *Macon* and *Savannah*. **Midway** (Liberty) is midway between *Savannah* and *Darien*. It was settled in 1695 by Puritan settlers who wanted to do missionary work with the Native Indians.

Between (Walton) sits between *Loganville* and *Monroe*, the two largest cities in the county, and between *Athens* and *Atlanta*, two of the largest cities in the state. Early townsfolk struggled with the challenge of choosing a new name, selecting the simplest and most obvious one, based on its location. Author Joshilyn Jackson named one of her books *Between Georgia.* Her Between is a fictitious town, the name referring to the conflict within the main character. She had to make the difficult choice between a rock and a hard place, meaning her biological or her adopted families.

Toonigh (Cherokee) is more commonly known as *Lebanon*, but the original railroad name is Toonigh, probably derived from a Cherokee word meaning "healer" or "curer." Toonowee was a lesser chief of the Cherokees. His name means "spring frog," but where's the legend of how the town got its name?

Toonigh was said to be "too nigh" Woodstock and Holly Springs to become a full-fledged town on its own. Another legend says that the train station building was assembled elsewhere, delivered on a flatbed truck and set "too nigh" to the railroad track. When a flatcar was brought to the train station and was set beside the track, one man walked down the track to see that it was not too close. If too close, he kept calling, "Too nigh, too nigh." Thus, the town became Toonigh.

Plum Nelly (Dade) is not actually a town, but a farm, located near *Rising Fawn*, Georgia. (See chapter 4.) The place was given this name because it is "plum" out of Tennessee and "nelly" out of Georgia.

The farm hosted a two-acre crafts center owned by artist Fannie Mennen, who was known for her annual "clothesline" art show, which was held the second weekend in October for twenty-six years through 1974. Known for her tireless commitment to her work and the arts community, her clothesline show attracted three hundred visitors the first year and grew to an attendance of twenty thousand. The two-day outdoor event represented some of the finest arts and crafts in the region. After her death in 1995, the New Salem Mountain Festival and Community Center continued her tradition. The Plum Nelly shop, now under its fourth owner, continues to sell high-quality work of regional artists.

3

TOWNS NAMED FOR WOMEN

Towns named for men who were politicians, generals, postmasters and engineers are a dime a dozen and could fill up this book and more. But towns named for women who were daughters, granddaughters, wives, sisters, postmistresses and town leaders are another story and deserve their own chapter.

We'll start with the capital city of Georgia, **Atlanta** (Fulton County), originally known as *Standing Peach Tree*. It also may have been *Pitch Tree*, mispronounced as "peach" by the native residents. Both pine trees that produce pitch or sap and peach trees that produce peaches were prominent in the area then and now. According to folklore, a tall and prominent pine or pitch tree was struck by lightning, causing the sap to run down the trunk. Thus, the name of the area became Pitch Tree. But an early postmaster says that there was a huge mound of earth that bore a big peach tree on its top. It's unusual for a singular peach tree to grow on a mound. Peaches grow in groves. The name *Peachtree*, and not Pitchtree, survived and is a common name, with minor variations, for streets in Atlanta. Letters are sometimes addressed to Peachtree Street, USA, and somehow manage to reach their destination.

The village name evolved into Whitehall, named for the white pioneers settling in the area. In the 1830s, the railroads came, with the Western and Atlantic Railroad officials deciding that Whitehall would be a good place to terminate the line. But they changed the name *Whitehall* to *Terminus*. (I'm getting to the woman part.)

Terminus was not considered a proper name for a town, especially one on the rise as a major railroad hub. After some discussion, Governor Wilson Lumpkin—one-time general manager of the Western and Atlantic—liked the name *Marthasville* for the town. It would honor his sixteen-year-old daughter, Martha. That name lasted only two years. It was too long, was a mouthful and didn't do justice to the up-and-coming railroad hub and future metropolis. But what would be the new name?

"Eureka, I've found it!" said J. Edgar Thompson, a chief engineer of the Western and Atlantic Railroad. He suggested the name *Atlanta*, a coined feminine version of *Atlantic*, the name of the rail line. And there you have it.

But there's more to the story and more about the legacy of Martha Lumpkin, now a Compton. Her father claimed that her middle name was Atalanta, for the Greek goddess of athleticism, being that Martha showed her athleticism by walking at an early age. There was proof in the family Bible, or perhaps manufactured proof. But how Atalanta really became Atlanta is anyone's guess. Martha Compton would go to her grave claiming the city of Atlanta was twice named for her.

Marietta (Cobb) is a large, historic city in Cobb County and considered part of metro Atlanta. Called the "Gem City of the South," it was made the county seat in the 1830s. It depends on whom you talk to, but it's generally said the name came from the wife of Georgia Supreme Court judge and U.S. senator Thomas W. Cobb, for whom the county is named. His wife's name was Mary. If this is the case, Judge Cobb would have the honor of having the county named for him and the county's largest city named for his wife.

Another story claims the town was named for two legendary "charming young ladies" whose Christian names were Mary and Etta, with Marietta being a coined combination of the two names.

Alpharetta (Fulton) is part of the northern suburban sprawl of Atlanta. Incorporated in 1858, it was originally called *New Prospect Campground*. The name Alpharetta has two origin stories of interest. The more mundane story says it is a coined name after the first letter of the Greek alphabet. It was a pragmatic decision, as local businesses could use the name to precede their competitors alphabetically in the Yellow Pages.

The more interesting story is that the name is a variant of Alfarata, a fictional Indian girl who sings the praises of her warrior lover as she travels along the Juniata River. Located in Pennsylvania, the river was the site of many bloody conflicts between white settlers and Native Americans.

Marion Dix Sullivan wrote a song about this Indian maiden called "The Blue Juniata," popular in the nineteenth century. Mark Twain referenced the song in his autobiography. Laura Ingalls Wilder in *Little House on the Prairie* wrote that her parents sang it to her as a lullaby, even though it filled her head with questions about the treatment of Native Americans. William Tecumseh Sherman was also said to love the tune. Roy Rogers and the early Sons of the Pioneers recorded a version in 1937.

It was the first commercially successful song written by an American woman. This is a verse from the song.

> *Bold is my warrior good,*
> *The love of Alfarata,*
> *Proud waves his snowy plume*
> *Along the Juniata.*
> *Soft and low he speaks to me,*
> *And then, his war-cry sounding,*
> *Rings his voice in thunder loud,*
> *From height to height resounding.*

There will be more Indian legend love stories in chapter 4.

Lula (Hall County), sometimes spelled Lulah, was named for the daughter of Ferdinand Phinizy of Athens, Georgia. Some say the town was named for the daughter of railroad builder R.L. Moss of Athens, but the arrow points to Lula Phinizy, eventual wife of Dr. A.W. Calhoun, noted occulist of Atlanta.

Civil engineers Joel Hurt and his brother Fletcher were admirers of Lula and recommended her name be used for the town that completed the rail spur from Athens.

The photo of the author in the oversized rocking chair was taken on Lula Road in Lula, at milepost 10 on Highway 52, going toward Clermont. It's a fun chair to sit in, take a photo and wave to passing tourists. But there aren't many cars that go by, so bring a book to read.

Camilla (Mitchell) is named for Camilla Mitchell, the nineteen-year-old daughter of Revolutionary War hero General Henry Mitchell.

Her namesake town grew infamous for an 1868 riot during the Reconstruction era involving three hundred freedmen, who would not be guaranteed the right to vote until 1869 with the ratification of the Fifteenth Amendment. Republican political candidates marched to the town's courthouse square. The local sheriff and "citizens committee" warned the

The author sitting in a large rocking chair in Lula. *Photo by Robert Gaare.*

black and white activists and ordered them to forfeit their guns. (Carrying weapons on one's person was customary at the time.) The marchers refused and continued to the courthouse, where they were fired upon by a group of local whites who had been quickly deputized. An estimated fifty to seventy-five African American marchers were killed or wounded. Over the next two weeks, citizen vigilantes continued to roam the county, threatening blacks with death if they tried to vote. This was the beginning of the Jim Crow era in the South. Laws from this time stayed on the books for the next one hundred years.

Camilla experienced another race riot in July 1962, when a group of civil rights activists tried to visit their fellow demonstrators who had been jailed. Marion King, pregnant wife of the leader of the Albany Georgia Movement, was beaten, kicked unconscious and subsequently suffered a miscarriage. Her story is documented in a song, "Camilla," by Decatur, Georgia resident Caroline Herring.

Of note, the town was struck by two disastrous tornadoes in 2000 and 2003.

The Camilla of today boasts many fun festivals, including the Gnat Days of Summer on the first Saturday in May to honor that summer scourge insect. Another fun event is the Pet Valentine Costume Contest.

Actress Kate Claxton, Claxton, Georgia's namesake. *Library of Congress.*

Alma (Bacon), known as "Georgia's Blueberry Capital," hosts a three-day festival each June. A group of residents in the early 1900s was trying to decide what to name the town. A Mr. Sheridan, a drummer (another term for a salesman), arrived from Macon with a name suggestion—Alma—after his wife. Is this the real reason the town was named Alma, or is it because it's a coined name from the first letters of the four Georgia capitals: Augusta, Louisville, Milledgeville and Atlanta?

Claxton (Evans) is the town that wanted to be named *Hendricks*, but postal officials in D.C. declined to approve the name, as there was already a post office in Upson County operating under that name. Two new names were submitted: Jenny and Claxton. Postal officials agreed on Claxton.

Some say the town is named for Kate Claxton, a popular actress at the time of the city's founding. She made her first appearance on stage in 1870 and was famous for being one of the best "emotional actresses" of the time. That talent was put to the most extreme test when she was performing *The Two Orphans* on December 5, 1876, at the Brooklyn Theatre in New York. A fire broke out that killed 278 people. The actress survived to have the Georgia town named after her. Others say the town was named to honor Philander Priestly Claxton, a noted educator of the time.

No matter how Claxton got its name, the town is known for fruitcake. Claxton is the "Fruitcake Capital of the World." Albert Parker started a bakery specializing in a fruit-and-nut cake for Christmas that became locally famous. But when the local Civitan Club decided the fruitcake would make an ideal fundraiser, that's when the cake filled with sugared fruit and nuts came to fame. More than one thousand organizations now sell the treat. Parker's Claxton Bakery is a fifty-thousand-square-foot facility that covers

Signage at the large block that contains the home of the Claxton Fruit Cake Bakery. *Photo by Robert Gaare.*

a city block. Inside are five massive ovens capable of producing eighty-six thousand pounds of cake daily that is shipped all over the world.

Supposedly the cake has a shelf life of four months, but humorist Lewis Grizzard claimed there is really only one fruitcake in existence and we just pass it around. One year, a Savannah radio station held a contest to drop, toss and catapult unwanted fruitcakes to see which made the best splatter. But contest rules prohibited destruction of Claxton fruitcakes. Those are sacred. Claxton people said those substandard fruitcake knockoffs deserved to be thrown away anyway. John Womble, third-generation operator of the Georgia Fruit Cake Company, even collects fruitcake gags and jokes. Once, he printed a picture of the "Attack of the Killer Fruitcake" on the cover of his family Christmas card.

Claxton also hosts the annual Rattlesnake Roundup, held the second weekend in March. To my knowledge, no rattlesnakes are thrown or passed around.

Lavonia (Franklin) is named for Lavonia Jones, the wife of John H. Jones, president of the Elberton Airline Railroad. The town may be named for a woman, but its four main streets are named for the four town promoters: J.H. Jones, J.H. Grogan, J.H. Vickery and T.J. Bowman.

A side story about Lavonia involves a queen of a gypsy clan who died nearby in 1908 and was buried in Burgess Cemetery in Lavonia. Born in England, this gypsy queen lived in the United States for almost fifty years. For many subsequent years after her death, her gypsy clan would bring the remains of other clan members to be buried in graves next to their queen. They would arrive in limousines with leopard-skin upholstery. The gypsies were personally adorned with oodles of diamonds. The last of the queen's clan to make a pilgrimage to Burgess was reported in the 1930s.

Lizella (Bibb) is pronounced Lye-zella and is an unincorporated community that was first called *Warrior*. A pioneer settler and first postmaster, James A Eubanks, needed to change the name, as there was already a Warrior, Georgia. He felt it would make him look conceited to use his last name, Eubanks, so he decided to name the town after his daughters. Unable to favor one over the other, he coined the name Lizella after both of them—Lizzy and Ella Eubanks.

Helen (White) was so named in 1913 after the daughter of the railway surveyor of the Gainesville and Northwestern Railroad. Helen was an early gold-mining town and part of the Georgia gold rush belt. A prominent lumber company was in operation until the 1930s. By the 1960s, there was

A typical gypsy funeral and burial, an annual pilgrimage. *Library of Congress.*

nothing left of the booming town except its history and a dreary row of concrete block structures.

In 1968, a local businessman called together other town leaders to discuss a way to revive the town. An artist, who had been stationed in Germany, began to sketch the town as a German village, adding gingerbread trims, murals and colors to resemble an Alpine façade. In a few years, the town of Helen turned into Bavaria, Georgia. It hosts millions of visitors annually, particularly during Oktoberfest.

Ila (Madison) was originally called *O'Possum* but then changed to Ila, in honor of a pretty little girl of the community. It also may have been derived from a Choctaw word meaning "dead." Is it a dead city? No. It's not dead, as the 2000 Census lists a population of 328.

Widow's Fool (Bibb) is supposedly named after a prominent Cherokee woman, the wife of Fool, a fighting chief in Tennessee who lived in the vicinity of Rome, Georgia, where he operated a ferry. It was said he was a man with "erratic behavior" when it came to wooing widows. The issue remains questionable: Was the town named for his wife, who, as a widow,

A typical building and street view in Helen, Georgia's Alpine Village. *Photo by Robert Gaare.*

was wooed and caught by him? Or was the town named for him because he acted foolishly around widows? The choice is yours.

Briefly, here are a few more towns named for women, but probably not all.

Jennie (Evans) is named for Jennie Grice, later Mrs. David Bradley and daughter of the town's postmaster.

Cordele (Crisp) is named in honor of the oldest daughter of Colonel Samuel Hawkins, president of the Savannah, Americus, and Montgomery (SAM) Railroad. Cordele calls itself the "Watermelon Capital of the World."

Stellaville (Jefferson) was first known as *Sisterville*, for the sister of prominent citizen John Brinson, but it switched to Stellaville, for her first name.

Roberta (Crawford) was originally called *New Knoxville*. When the rails came to town, a new train station was built, and so was a new town. Hiram David McCrary let the railroad use part of his land and was given naming rights to the town. He named the town Roberta, for his seven-year-old daughter.

Doraville (DeKalb) was named for Dora Jack, the daughter of—you guessed it—an official of the Southern Railway.

Ruth (Greene) was named for the first postmistress, Ruth Williams.

Rebecca (Turner) was named for Rebecca Clark, daughter of Zach Clark, head of a prominent Turner County family.

Vidalia (Toombs) was named for the daughter of—you guessed it again—an early railroad promoter. (There's more on Vidalia in chapter 16.)

Leslie (Sumter) was named for Leslie Bailey, who was described as "a lovely young girl." Leslie houses the Georgia Rural Telephone Museum.

Kinderlou (Lowndes) is named for the sister of dairy farmer and prominent first citizen George McRee. She had been a mother to his three sons. *Kinder* is German for "children," and *Lou* comes from her first name, Louisa.

Ellabell (Bryan) is an unincorporated community named by John A. Morrison, who was married to Iola Bell Morrison. One of their children was Ellabell Morrison, who became the town's namesake.

Daisy (Evans) was intended to be named *Conley* for the Reverend W.F. Conley, a Methodist minister, but the U.S. Postal Office (USPO) rejected this name because another town had already claimed it. So the townspeople decided on the name Daisy, for Daisy Leola Edwards, daughter of Thomas Jefferson Edwards and granddaughter of Reverend Conley.

Euharlee (Bartow) derived its meaning from the Indian name Eufaula, meaning, "she laughs as she runs."

Isabella/Isabella Station (Worth) are really two different towns, so near to each other that they eventually merged into the town of *Sylvester* in the late 1800s. Isabella was several miles away and was the name of a railroad station, important to area farmers because crops and supplies were shipped in and out from there.

Major William A. Harris was instrumental to the naming of Isabella. He gave the county the name of Worth, in honor of his commander in the Mexican War, General William Jenkins Worth, and named the once county seat, Isabella, for the general's wife, Margaret Isabella Stafford. She preferred the name Isabella over Margaret. In 1879, the courthouse burned. It was rebuilt, then it burned again in 1893. By this time, Isabella and Isabella Station were renamed Sylvester, based on two Latin names: *silva*, meaning "woods," and *vaster*, meaning "your."

We end this chapter with a familiar story and a recipe. **Juliette** (Monroe) is named for Juliette McCracken, the daughter of the railroad engineer (an all too familiar story by now) who built the railroad through the town. The town's real claim to fame is the Whistle Stop Café, the central location in the popular movie *Fried Green Tomatoes*, based on the book by Fannie Flagg. Although the book's setting was Alabama, the movie was filmed in Juliette, Georgia. After the movie finished filming, the sets were moved to a tourist district here, where you can still eat fried green tomatoes made using Sipsey's recipe.

To quote a line from the movie, "Oh what I wouldn't give for a plate of fried green tomatoes." You can make your own, for Sipsey's recipe is quite simple: sliced green tomatoes, salt and pepper to taste and cornmeal coating, then it is cooked in bacon fat. Apparently, it's the bacon fat that makes them taste good and authentic.

4

FROM CUSSETA TO SAUTEE-NACOOCHEE

NATIVE AMERICAN PLACE-NAMES

Native American place-names are everywhere in Georgia. Being the first residents, the Cherokee, Creek and Seminole influences are wide ranging. Indian names are often the original names of towns, but in other cases the Indian names have been Anglicized. There are far too many Indian place-names to mention in this chapter, so a few representative samples as well as a few legends are all that have been listed.

Cusseta (Chattahoochee) is a name derived from the Muscogee word meaning "a trading place," with Cusseta town meaning "White Peace Town." It was the largest trading post for the Muscogee and mentioned in William Bartram's *Travels*.

Settingdown Village (Forsyth) was named for the Cherokee chief Setten Down, so named because he allowed some of the white settlers to "set down" and live peaceably near his village.

Attapulgus (Decatur) was once called *Hack*, then it became the *Borough of Pleasant Grove*. There are many spelling variations of Attapulgus, meaning "dogwood grove" or "boring holes in wood to make a fire." Attapulgite is a mineral found in clay in this area. The term *Attapulgus* is found four times as a Georgia place-name and sometimes refers to a group of natives in its plural form.

Three Notch (Decatur), sometimes known as *Three Chops*, was named for the marks of an early trail of the 1800s with three notches on trees. Similarly named was **Chopped Oak** (Habersham), an early rendezvous point where many Indian trails crossed. The Indians recorded trophies in battles by making a gash in a great oak tree for every scalp taken. There were so many gashes in the tree, called the Chopped Oak, that the region became a nightmare for white settlers.

Wahoo/Burning Bush (Lumpkin) was a common name. *Wahoo* is the Dakota word for "burning bush." Arrow-wood or burning bush is the name of a shrubby bush with brilliant fall foliage. The name may allude to Exodus 3 in the Bible, in which God appears to Moses in a bush that, while on fire, does not burn up.

Chief Wahoo was the mascot/logo for the Cleveland Indians baseball team until it was considered derogatory to Native Americans. The new mascot is Bacon, for bacon on a stick, a popular concession in the ballpark. It remains to be seen if pigs will squeal over that.

The Logs: **Cherry Log** (Gilmer), **Pine Log** (Bartow) and **Hickory Log** (Bartow) were all once occupied by Cherokees and renamed by the settlers for creek crossings made from local felled trees. **Pine Log** was once popularly called Possum Trot or simply Trot. Supposedly, the Spanish explorer Hernando de Soto visited the village and was amazed at the skills of the Cherokee women in running the village while the men were out hunting or making war. Later, Benjamin Hawkins was sent by the president to be the federal Indian agent and was also impressed with the much-civilized Cherokees. Much civilized or not, they were still removed from the state by the mid-1830s.

Cherry Log (Gilmer) refers to a cherry log laid across the creek for a foot log, placed by the Cherokees prior to their removal from the county in 1836. Cherry trees are still abundant up and down the side of the North Georgia Mountains.

The Gilmer Historical Society tells the humorous story of resident Bud Searcy, who went out hunting with a party of his friends one night. All were carrying lanterns to light up a path in the woods. The friend in front nearly stepped on a band of wild hogs that had been sleeping in his path. Wild hogs were said to have been brought to Georgia by de Soto. (See more in chapter 16.)

The story continues with the hogs jumping up and charging. The men scattered right and left, climbing small trees to get away from the wild hogs. After the hogs quieted down and strolled away, Bud called out to his friends to bring him a light to help him get down from the tree. His friends found him sitting flat on the ground with his arms and legs locked around a small seedling. He had been sitting on the ground the entire time in the midst of the wild, chasing boars and thought he had climbed up a tree. Why didn't

The Cherry Log Post Office, located on the railroad tracks. *Photo by Robert Gaare.*

the hogs bite him? His friends said the answer was quite simple: The wild boars must have mistaken him for one of them.

Cherry Log is the home of **Expedition: Bigfoot, the Sasquatch Museum,** one of only two such museums in the country, created in 2016 as a labor of love by museum owner David Bakara and his wife, Malinda. The museum is dedicated to Bigfoot legends and research. As you enter through the front porch, you'll hear Indiana Jones–type movie music, setting the stage for an ominous adventure. You'll see a wall of photos of the Bigfoot researchers and then a short film asking you to enter with an open mind.

People who've seen the Sasquatch have had life-changing experiences. Although there is no conclusive scientific evidence that Bigfoot creatures exist, there are thousands of stories of sightings, many in Georgia. There's a seventeen-minute film in the Bigfoot theater, talking about mostly Kentucky sightings of the giant half man / half beast creature, varying in size from three hundred to one thousand pounds, being six to ten feet tall, with black, silvery white or reddish brown fur, a prominent brow, slits for a nose, long arms, huge hands and a face like a man's. There's a quote above the screen: "It's the glory of God to conceal a thing, but the honor of Kings to search out a matter" (Proverbs 25:2).

The author looking at a Bigfoot face to face. *Photo by Robert Gaare.*

Then you'll hear legends of the Sasquatch, who perhaps originated from an Indian "beauty and the beast" story. A small girl befriended the big beast, who showed her the shadows dancing on the wall caused by the firelight. She was fascinated with the shadows and his stories, but her family forbade her to go see the beast again. Missing her, he came and took her away. The family chased after them. Her face was scratched from low-lying branches; the rain made her cold; she was scared. Her pain touched his heart, so he brought her back to her people. They made him promise never to see her again. As a result, he had to hide from humans and no longer share his wonderful shadow stories. He's been hiding ever since.

The entrance to the Bigfoot Museum in Cherry Log. *Photo by Robert Gaare.*

The Native Americans have over eighty different names for Sasquatch. He has been seen in various forms all over the world for many, many years. Some people make it their life's mission to track him down—at least one of him. A good many sightings have been reported in White County, Georgia, near where the museum is located.

After seeing exhibits, hearing tales of sightings and viewing hand and footprints of the beast, will you leave the museum a believer? You'll certainly leave with your head full of scary stories and, maybe, your arms carrying a cute little stuffed Sasquatch from the gift shop. The two somehow don't seem to go together.

Licklog (Lumpkin) was an old salting place for cattle drives. Troughs were cut into the logs and salt put in for the animals. Cattle drivers would salt up the animals to increase their thirst and their weight before selling them or taking them to the slaughterhouse to make more money. The phrase "down to the lick log" refers to this second-to-last-stop for cattle before their demise.

Buffalo Lick (Greene) was also known as the Lick, named for a deposit of fossil salts and wild herbs that attracted buffaloes. Buffaloes came to lick the salt from the gray clay, which provided a soothing antacid for bison bellies. Yes, Georgia was once inhabited by buffaloes.

Talking Rock (Pickens) proudly boasts that it is the third-smallest town in the state. How did the name come about? Again, there are several stories. One says that Irishmen building the railroad left money on a big rock for natives to take and, in return, leave jugs of whiskey. The area became known as Talking Rock.

Some say it was named for a rocky cliff feeding into a stream that produced peculiar echoes as the water rolled down the rocks. Others say it was so named from a story about a rock that talked and that was used by the natives to play tricks on one another. Still another story comes from the Cherokee name and translation, which means "the talker" or "place of the talker." Townspeople would sit on the rocks and talk to their neighbors. Perhaps this last version of the place-name story is the real one.

Rock Pile (Dawson) was so named because early travelers and herd drivers tossed rocks onto a pile beside the road as a good luck gesture. It meant you would live to see that spot again.

Another rock pile story involves **Stonepile Gap** (White). What looks like an ordinary pile of rocks on U.S. Highway 19 and State Road 60 are rocks that sit on top of the grave of a Cherokee princess named Trahlyta. Although she was called a princess, the Cherokees technically did not have princesses. Trahlyta loved the forests and mountains of North Georgia so much that she wanted to live there forever. She also wanted to stay young and beautiful forever. So, she sought out the witch of Cedar Mountain, who told her that the secret to staying young and beautiful was to drink from the spring; then, her wish would come true. She did this, and her wish came true—and it would last as long as she kept drinking from the spring. Word of her beauty spread, but so did word that she had discovered a fountain of youth. Spanish explorer Hernando de Soto sent some of his men to hunt for this spring, but they never found it…in Georgia.

Back to Trahlyta. A Cherokee warrior named Wahsega kidnapped her to be his bride and took her far away from her home and her spring. She begged him to let her go back to her beloved mountains. He did not. Her strength and beauty began to fade, and she died. Upon her death, her husband finally granted her last wish and took her home to be buried. Passersby drop a stone on her grave for good fortune.

Seekers of good fortune have dropped one rock at a time on her grave over a number of years, turning it into a pile of stones making up Stonepile

The pile of rocks covering Cherokee Princess Trahlyta's grave off Highway 19 and State Road 60. Beware if you remove one! *Photo by Robert Gaare.*

Gap. A curse remains that anyone taking a stone from the pile will incur the wrath of the witch of Cedar Mountain. A marker by her grave offers these words of advice:

Pass not by, Stranger! Stop! Silently bare your head, drop a stone upon her grave, and make a wish straight from your heart. The spirit of Eternal Youth and happiness hovers nearby to grant the wishes of all who love the hills and valleys of her native home.

This curse has been tested. The Georgia Department of Highways set out to relocate the grave, twice, to make road construction more convenient. On both occasions, serious accidents occurred. Tractors were wrecked, and workmen were injured. Finally, it was agreed to leave the rock pile alone except for passersby who continue to leave rocks on the pile, many with messages on them.

What about Trahlyta's fountain of youth? Has anyone ever found it? It's thought that the springs in question are Porter Springs. A Spanish helmet was found close to the springs, offering evidence of this as the place where de Soto's men searched for the magical waters. Joseph H. McKee, a Methodist preacher who dabbled in real estate, took note of Porter Springs in the 1860s. He tested the water and found it contained an abundance of therapeutic minerals. He publicized his findings, and people seeking cures for rheumatism, dyspepsia, dropsy and other ailments flocked to the springs. They would camp nearby, bathe in the waters and take home gallons of the liquid. A hotel was constructed in the area and became a thriving resort, thanks to the legend of Trahlyta and the fountain of youth. The hotel burned in the early 1900s, but the spring waters continue to flow. (See stories of more Georgia springs in chapter 18.)

Pocotaligo (Madison) is pronounced "Pokey Tally go." It's a Native American name for "big gathering place town" or "border town." But legends tell a different story of the name. A local legend tells of a balky mule that would only "go" if you poked his tail. Another variation in the story is of a closed-up turtle. The sure-fire method to make him open up his shell and move was to poke his tail. It's your choice which version to go by.

Buzzard's Roost (Union) comes from a Cherokee creation story about a flight from the upper world by a great buzzard who was seeking a site for the animals of his world. His world was too crowded. At the time, there was a huge flood on earth. As he flew closer to the earth, the flapping of his wings caused the waters to dry. The beating of his wings in the mud caused the mountains to form where the buzzard finally found a place to roost. Even today, that area is known as Buzzard's Roost.

Frogtown (Union) was called *Walasiyi*, meaning "the great frog." Walasiyi was the frog god of the Cherokees.

Ellijay (Gilmer) is the apple capital of Georgia. The name comes from the Cherokee word meaning "new ground" or "green place." Former president Jimmy Carter has a log cabin and second home here.

Rising Fawn (Dade) is an example of Anglicizing a Native American name and changing it into a more pleasant-sounding or easier-to-pronounce English one. Literal translations resulted in names like Old Bear Guts, Rottenwood, Noisy, Bullhead and Pigeon on the Roost. In the case of Rising Fawn, the literal translation from the Cherokee *Agi na gi li* is "young, he is rising," which is much more pleasant than "Pigeon on the Roost" or "Old Bear Guts."

The name of the town has been listed as Rising Town and Rising Farm, but Rising Fawn has stuck. According to legend, the Cherokees named their newborns after the first thing they saw at the child's birth. In this case, it was a fawn seeming to rise from its mother's side. There were plenty of male Cherokees who had this name. But legend says there was a Cherokee princess named Rising Fawn. (Remember that Cherokees did not have princesses.) Storytellers love to use an Indian maiden in their tales, usually involving a tragic love story; but there is no substance to this claim.

Today's Rising Fawn is a well-known location for chainsaw wood carvers and clay studios. Artists, artisans and musicians live in the mountains and are involved in several popular arts and crafts festivals, like the Howard Finster Art Festival and the nearby Plum Nelly Festival (featured in chapter 2).

Doctortown (Wayne) is the only site on the Altamaha River that retains its old Indian name. It is derived from a Muscogee Indian word, *Alekcha* or *Aixcha*, which translates to "doctor." A lower Creek Indian chief called Alleck ("doctor") resided near here. It is thought to have been the site of an Indian medicine town. But it is no more.

For many years, the only road and rail crossing of the coastal plain was here, making Doctortown a vital shipping and travel point. During World War II, Doctortown was still functioning. The Coast Guard posted at bridges here to ward off the threat of German sabotage. Today, Doctortown is a ghost town, with access cut off by the world's largest pulp mill, Rayonier Performance Fibers, in Jessup. It is the largest cellulose specialties plant in the world.

Quill (Gilmer) is a community near Ellijay named for a Cherokee scribe who rushed to teach the Sequoyan alphabet to his people in the hopes that, through a written language, the Cherokee people could be saved. Alas, the Cherokees were removed from Georgia in the wake of the Indian Removal Act of 1830, sending them on the perilous Trail of Tears into Oklahoma Territory. One quarter of the Cherokees died on this trail.

Ola (Henry) is an Indian word meaning "the other side." Ola is the suffix to the names of many Indian towns, like Osceola, Amicalolola and Yahoola.

Nahunta (Brantley) is derived from the Iroquoian word meaning "tall trees." Others say it's based on a colloquialism that comes from railroad maps and a sign that read "N.A. Hunter Siding."

Ball Ground (Cherokee) represents the site of very early Cherokee ball games, originally called chunkey. A round stone was carved into the shape of a disc and was rolled across the playing area until it stopped. The players competed in pairs, throwing a spear-like wooden pole six to eight feet long at the disc. The player whose stick was closest to the chunkey stone was declared the winner of that point.

By 1775, there was nothing left of these villages and mounds but ruins. But the game continued. The Cherokee called it "the little brother of war" or simply "ball game," similar to our modern game of lacrosse. It became a contact sport with ball sticks fashioned of bent hickory forming a loop at one end in which a web of leather or sinew was attached. It looked similar to a war club. The ball was made of leather stuffed with hair. Certain balls held objects hidden inside. Through sympathetic magic, the properties of parts of birds or animals were transferred to the ball itself.

It was a violation to use your hands to handle the ball, but it was okay to put the ball in your mouth. (How it got there without using one's hand is anybody's guess.) The playing field might cover many acres, and the game might last many days. Two sticks were driven into the ground as a goal post. The ball needed to go between the posts to score a goal. In the Cherokee/Choctaw/Creek version of the game, players carried the ball cupped between the two sticks. The ball was in the air most of the time, with players able to catch the ball in midair with the two sticks. A player had to periodically sprint long distances at top speed.

Each team had a medicine man or shaman who infused magic and ritual into the game. He made a fire and offered prayers and songs to bless his team and increase its chances of victory. By using magic, he laid a curse on the opposing team. Prior to a match, the players observed a strict diet and even sexual abstinence and were sequestered in training camps. "Going to the water" meant immersing themselves and their playing sticks seven times, like a Christian baptism, and singing a special song. The sticks were doctored with special medicine during the immersion.

Then there was the process of scarification before the game. A shaman would scratch the player's skin with a special instrument made of turkey bones to draw blood, removing the bad blood, and psyching up the player. There were referees and two switchers who carried wooden whips for the purpose of disciplining a player for rule infractions. Players could be tackled. The action often became violent, the games degenerating into wrestling matches and often resulting in bloodshed and injury, a confusing free-for-all. Breaking of heads or limbs or choking your opponent when excited was part of the game but was ruled out around 1848. Before that, anything went.

The game was ranked next to war as the manliest occupation. The victory or defeat was attributed to the success of the medicine men, who developed the strategies. Nearly all of the games were wagered on.

Ball Ground, Georgia, was one of the playing sites. The game traveled with the Cherokees and Creeks as they were forced to relocate to Oklahoma.

Tallulah Falls (Rabun) is a town and the name of a major waterfall called the "Niagara of the South." The name originated from the Choctaw, meaning "bell," or from the Cherokee for "terrible," or from the Cherokee phrase *tu lu lu li*, meaning "the frogs are here." Other possibilities are the Cherokee *Aa lu lu*, meaning "unfinished," the Cherokee for "rock" or maybe as a tribute to the actress Tallulah Bankhead. Or is the name simply untranslatable?

In the early 1800s, the area blossomed into a retreat for wealthy travelers who wanted to view the spectacular scenery and six major waterfalls that feed into the gorge. People also enjoyed hearing the legends. The regional Indians believed a race of little people called the Uyundi Tsundi dwelled in the caves and crevices of the gorge. Strong warriors who wandered into the domain of these magical little people never returned. They simply disappeared. The Cherokee rarely descended into the gorge for this very reason.

In July 1886, the first aerialist/tightrope walker, J.A. St. John, known as "Professor Leon," attempted to cross the gorge on a highwire, but there was a snap, and halfway across, the wire began to sway. The line had been cut. With the help of supporters, he made it across.

Some eighty-four years later, in 1970, the "Great Wallenda," Karl Wallenda, one of the famous Wallenda brothers, crossed the gorge in

Karl Wallenda doing a handstand while crossing Tallulah Gorge. *Stock photo.*

eighteen minutes, entertaining the crowd by doing two handstands while crossing. The feat was witnessed by some twenty-four thousand spectators and filmed by the BBC. His great-grandson planned to re-create the feat in 2015 but backed out due to technical reasons.

In 1913, the Georgia Railway and Power Company built Tallulah Falls Dam to tame the Niagara of the South and harness its river power to generate electricity. Coupled with a fire in 1921, Tallulah Falls never recovered. Today, however, there are seasonal releases of water through the gorge, and visitors are allowed to paddle down the white waters. Hikers can often be seeing walking the gorge (a major feather in anyone's cap) and crossing a majestic suspension bridge.

We'll conclude this chapter with the Romeo and Juliet love story of Sautee and Nacoochee, the namesakes for the town **Sautee-Nacoochee**, (White County). They were from rival tribes, Cherokee and Chickasaw. The two tribes would often engage in acts of war. During one time of peace, a small band of Chickasaws was permitted to cross into Cherokee land so long as they didn't deviate from the Unicoi Trail, an old Indian trading path from Augusta, Georgia, to east Tennessee. The visitors stopped to rest where the two valleys met and rested under a giant oak tree.

Curious Cherokees moved closer to get a look at their enemy. One Cherokee curiosity seeker was Nacoochee, daughter of a chief. One visiting Chickasaw was Sautee, a chief's son who dreamt of the day when

The mound at Sautee-Nachoochee that legend says is the grave site of the lovers Sautee and Nacoochee. *Library of Congress.*

he would become chief and could negotiate a peace with the Cherokees. Without a word spoken between them, their eyes met and, voila! The magic of love.

That night, Nacoochee stole away to meet with Sautee under this same giant oak. Hopelessly in love by then, they broke the terms of the truce. Sautee thought their tryst might be the first step toward a lasting peace between the two nations. Surely their fathers would see how their love united the two tribes.

In the meantime, the two would flee to the nearby Yonah Mountains to a secret cave, where they could spend a few idyllic days. When the two finally confronted Chief Wahoo, Nacoochee's father, he was blind with rage, ordering Sautee thrown from the high cliffs of Yonah Mountain. Nacoochee was forced to watch. She broke from her father's hold to leap from the high cliff, following her lover. The two broken bodies were found in a final embrace at the foot of the mountain.

It was too late for Wahoo to approve of their great love. It was too late for him to break the warring with the Chickasaws. He had the two bodies laid to rest in a burial mound easily seen today at the junction of Georgia Highways 17 and 75. So that the tragedy would never be forgotten, Chief Wahoo renamed the two valleys Sautee and Nacoochee, jointly known as the town Sautee-Nacoochee.

(See more information about Sautee-Nacoochee in chapter 6.)

5

THAR'S GOLD IN THEM THAR HILLS!

G host Town **Auraria** (Lumpkin), located just south of Dahlonega, was the first gold-mining town in American history. The area was once widely and wildly populated by settlers in search of gold. The boom started in 1832 and lasted until 1848, when the gold rush started in California. First called *Deans*, then *Nuckollsville* (both after early settlers), then *Scuffle-Town*, Auraria was the name settled on, coined from the French word *aureate*, meaning "gold region," and the Latin word *aurum*, meaning "gold."

These were former Cherokee lands. Following the Gold Lottery of 1832, the area was opened to white settlers, who quickly created a gold rush boomtown with taverns, hotels, stores and law offices (much needed to settle the many disputes). Today, Auraria is a ghost town. When the gold mines stopped operating, so did the town. Auraria, the first gold-mine town in the United States, was also the first to go bust.

But it was not so in **Dahlonega** (Lumpkin), incorporated in 1833, taking over from Auraria as the county seat. Dahlonega is translated from the Cherokee meaning "golden color" or "yellow money." Formerly called *Mexico*, *New Mexico*, *Licklog* and *Headquarters*, it is here that the center of Georgia's historic gold-mining region was located.

And it is here that twenty-nine-year-old Benjamin Parks was deer hunting in 1828 and kicked up something that caught his eye. It was gold, of course.

In an 1894 interview with the *Atlanta Constitution*, Benjamin Parks said, "I went to him [Reverend Obarr who owned the land] and told him I

Site of the discovery of gold by Benjamin Parks in 1828 at the intersection of Calhoun Mine Road, four miles south of Dahlonega. *Photo by Robert Gaare.*

thought I could find gold on his place if he would give me a lease of it. He laughed, as though he did not believe me, and consented. So a lease for forty years was written out, the consideration of which was that I was to give him one fourth of the gold mined....I went over to the spot with a pan, and turning over some earth, it looked like the yellow of an egg. It was more than my eyes could believe. The news got abroad and such excitement you never saw. It seemed within a few days as if the whole world must have heard of it, for men came from every state I had ever heard of, acting like crazy men."

Reverend Robert Obarr, although a Baptist minister, was a "hard man and very desperate," according to Benjamin Parks. Obarr realized his great mistake in leasing the land and the other three quarters of the gold and tried every which way to intimidate Parks into giving up the lease. He failed every time.

Once, Obarr said, "Well the longest pole will knock off the persimmon." What he meant was that he intended to break the sluice gate to let out the water and wash away the gold. A scuffle ensued, and Obarr had Parks and his cohorts arrested. Then Obarr sold his share to a Judge Underwood, who then sold the land to Senator John C. Calhoun of South Carolina.

Benjamin Parks lost a fortune. As he put it, "Senator Calhoun wanted to buy my lease, and I sold it for what I thought was a good price. The very first month after the sale he took out 24,000 pennyweights of gold and then I was inclined to be as mad with him as Obarr had been with me. But that is the peculiarity of gold mining. You will go day after day exhausting your means and your strength until you give it up. Then the first man who touches the spot finds the gold the first opening he makes. It is just like gambling; all luck."

Soon, there were over fifteen thousand miners living in the area. Shanties were set up all over the county where whiskey was sold freely. The area was run by thieves, gamblers, murderers and quarrelsome drunks forming a lawless, ungovernable community.

It should be noted that the Cherokees in the area knew of the gold long before the whites did and had already set up gold mines. Many historians say that gold was by far the most important factor in the early pressure for the quick removal of the Cherokees. Before they left on the Trail of Tears in the early 1830s, the Cherokees purportedly hid their treasures in the mountains where the white men couldn't find them. And they never did.

Also of note, John C. Calhoun opened the Calhoun Mines with brother-in-law Thomas Clemson, who ran the mine. Part of the money that came from the mine was used to fund Clemson University.

Between 1828 and 1849, over $20 million in gold was mined in Dahlonega. The end of the era was marked in 1849 by the California gold rush, miners now traveling west to seek their fortunes. In 1886, mining in Dahlonega turned to the hydraulic system, operating until the Calhoun Mine went bankrupt in 1907. The new system turned out to be too expensive in comparison to the yield of gold. Gold mining has returned off and on and is now largely recreational for the tourists. But all the gold in the Dahlonega hills has not been played out. There's still a lot of gold hidden in the mountains by Indians or inaccessible due to Mother Nature and the elements.

The stop sign at Calhoun Mine Road at the site of Benjamin Parks's discovery of gold. The marker that used to be there is missing. *Photo by Robert Gaare.*

The entrance to Consolidated Gold Mines, where tourists can pan for gold in Dahlonega. *Photo by Robert Gaare.*

The Dahlonega Gold Museum on the town square is the state's oldest public building and holds a place in the National Register of Historic Places.

The Calhoun Mine is now privately owned and closed to the public. The marker is missing due to road construction, but a nearby resident and relative of Benjamin Parks's by marriage confirmed this was the site.

In 1958, a caravan of wagons from Dahlonega carried forty-three ounces of gold leaf, donated by the citizens of Lumpkin County, to be applied to the state capitol dome. The dome is lit by a torch held by the statue of Lady Liberty.

Two golden flowers, a dahlia and a daylily, have become the iconic symbols of Dahlonega and are on some of the city's logos, along with the words "It's pure gold."

It is said that there was gold mining in Union County long before the mining occurred in Lumpkin County. An old writing says that Uncle Bill Henderson's father, born and reared on Gumlog Creek, was the first to find gold in the **Gumlog** mines. He mischievously threw a rock at a girl who was hiding in a tree. The rock burst open and had gold in abundance in its core—the yellowest gold in the world. This is similar to Benjamin Park's story. At least $2 million worth of gold was taken from this area. The Union County Coosa mines stopped operating around 1900.

A side story, while we're talking about gold, is what happened to the gold of the Confederacy. The answer brings us to Georgia, of course, where Jefferson Davis, president of the Confederacy, was arrested near **Irwinville**. He was en route from Richmond (the capital of the Confederacy) to board a ship and flee to safety in Cuba. He hoped to find a foreign country to empathize with his plight.

The Davis family camped near Irwinville and was overtaken by members of the First and Fourth Michigan Cavalries. We won't delve too much into the story of whether Davis was taken away wearing a woman's shawl for the sake of his health or as a disguise. The answer always depends on which side you favor—North or South. But the story to follow here is the path of the Confederate gold.

When Jefferson Davis was told by General Robert E. Lee that the evacuation of Richmond was imminent, he was advised to leave and take the Confederate treasury with him. He and his party had until 8:00 p.m. to load the gold, valuables and cabinet members onto two trains that would travel on the only railroad line open to them. The first train held the Confederate officials; the second held the special cargo of about $700,000 in gold and hard currency. They had intended to deposit the treasure at

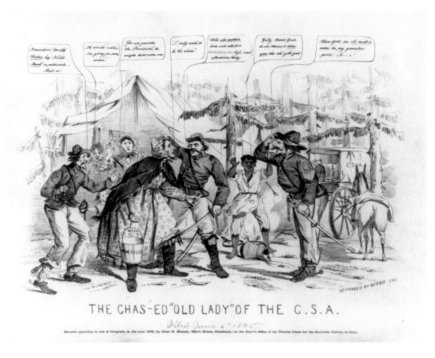

THE CHAS-ED "OLD LADY" OF THE C.S.A.

Print from a Union newspaper satirizing the capture of Jefferson Davis in Georgia. *Library of Congress.*

the Old U.S. Mint in Charlotte, North Carolina, but were forced to turn back when they met up with the U.S. Cavalry already in the area. They made alternate arrangements to head for Georgia.

In **Washington, Georgia**, named after George Washington, the cabinet of the Confederacy met for the last time. Secretary of War John C. Breckinridge and Brigadier General Basil Duke began to disperse the treasury in payments to meet the military payrolls. The balance of about $43,000 was placed in a vault at a local bank. Within days after the war ended, the funds were removed from the bank and began a return trip to Richmond in five wagons. The first night this wagon train stopped to make camp, it was robbed. The robbers stuffed the loot in their shirts, pants and boots, but the money leaked out, leaving a trail for a posse to follow. Almost all was recovered and transferred to Augusta, where ownership of the funds was tied up in courts until 1893.

As it turns out, there was no lost or hidden gold of the Confederacy. There was no other story to tell. But Martha Mizell Puckett, in her book *Snow White Sands*, tells of the Mumford family being the recipients of the leftover Confederate treasury, using the money to create an orphanage and college scholarships. Noble causes indeed, but the truth, most in the know say, is that, by the end, nothing remained in the coffers of the Confederate treasury except for its great, insurmountable debt.

6

LITTLE BROWN JUG, HOW I LOVE THEE

JUG TAVERNS, TOWNS AND POTTERY

From Vinegar Hill to Scantville, from Social Circle to Jug Tavern, and to all the Jug Towns and potters of Georgia, we pay tribute in this chapter.

Vinegar Hill (Walton) was a community possibly named for the early Irish settlers who remembered the Battle of Vinegar Hill between the Rebels and the British in 1798. But there's another story. Jasper Newton Smith, known as Jack, was born in 1833 in the Vinegar Hill area. As a young man, he worked at a local tavern, where he became concerned when an increasing number of guests stopped in for drinks. Would there be enough liquor to go around? No, he surmised, the demand would definitely exceed the supply. So he watered down the drinks and the whiskey bottles. To the dismay of the customers, the liquor turned to vinegar. To remind Jack Smith of his parsimony, his family's home was dubbed Vinegar Hill.

Eventually, the whole community came to be known by that name. Jasper/ Jack went on to become a wealthy brickmaker in Atlanta after General William Tecumseh Sherman's burning of the town. He continued to be a skinflint, known for his tightwad ways, throughout his life. His life-sized sculpture sits atop his mausoleum near the front gates of Oakland Cemetery, where he looks over the incoming visitors. I have more information about Jasper in my book for The History Press, *Historic Oakland Cemetery of Atlanta: Speaking Stones*.

Scantville (Carroll) has a similar story to Vinegar Hill's. The name refers to the habit of local bootleggers watering down the product so that the liquor was "scanty," but the water was not.

Photo of a sculpture of Jasper Newton Smith atop his mausoleum at Oakland Cemetery, Atlanta. *Photo by Ren Davis.*

Social Circle (Walton), settled in 1820, was a station for overland drives of livestock. The "Crackers" who came to town would swap stories and socialize while passing the jug. With the stimulation of a keg of spirits, the town was known for being a convivial spot and was therefore called Social Circle. To add to this tale, it is said that the town's founders were sitting around a drinking well, having a conversation, when a passerby noted, "This sure is a social circle."

Nicholsville or **Nickelsville** (Gordon) was sometimes called *Little Five Points* because the roads radiated in five different directions from here. The town was granted a liquor license in 1887 for the one and only store in the county that sold a drink of whiskey, and for only five cents. The name became Nickelsville or variations of that spelling. Some say the town was named for Lawrence Nichols, but that's the less interesting story.

Kings Bench (Franklin) was established in 1832 with William King Jr. as its first postmaster. Many towns were named for the first postmaster, but this one could have gotten its name for the large work benches in front of the store where liquor could be bought. On days when liquor and money were flowing freely—meaning, after every payday—the drinks were placed on large benches and sold to customers from there.

Jug Tavern (Barrow), when first settled, was called *The Jug*, because early settler Alonzo Draper said the shape of his land resembled a jug. The three-hundred-yard-wide field represented the body of the jug, the stacked timber its neck, and his house was the stopper. The circular body part was lined by a fifty-foot circle of timber used as a protection against Indians and wild animals.

The original name for the village was *Snodon*, renamed *Jug* and then renamed Jug Tavern. That name stuck until it became *Winder*, the name that is currently used.

Jug Tavern or Jug Tavern Crossroads was composed of two Indian trails that crossed near a tavern. More than likely, Jug Tavern got its name from a tavern owned by Captain Garland Reynold, from England, who built it on the side yard of his home. He could make "an honest penny" selling liquor. A large jug suspended from the rafters by a red ribbon marked the spot where food, lodging and all the whiskey a man could drink without taking

Print used for the logo of the Jug Tavern Railroad route connecting Gainesville and Social Circle. *Photo by Cathy Kaemmerlen, taken at the Bartow Museum.*

the jug from his lips was only ten cents. In 1884, it became the Jug Tavern Railroad route. Steam locomotives connected *Gainesville* and *Social Circle*, with stops at *Jug Tavern* and *Mulberry*, and at *Bethlehem*. This Jug Tavern route was symbolized with a large jug, suggesting Georgia hospitality and plenty of moonshine to fill the jug and the customer.

Winder (Barrow), formerly Jug Tavern, was created from parts of three counties: Walton, Jackson and Gwinnett. One story as to how the name Winder came to be involves a fight between two men. In three minutes' time, one of the men was shot in Jackson County, staggered wounded into Walton and fell dead in Gwinnett. It was said he "winded around" three counties before dying. Most people say the name Winder came from honoring railroad builder and manager John H. Winder.

So we have a repeating pattern…a more interesting folkore story of how a town got its name versus the town being named for a railroad engineer, railroad president or a general. I think we know which story is the one we'll remember and retell.

Barrow County is home to a historical museum, housed in the old Barrow County Jail. There are remnants of jugs—big and small—in the museum cases that date back to Jug Tavern days. The Barrow County Historical Society even had a "Jug drop" on New Year's Eve 2009. Fifty miniature jugs modeled after the original jug tavern jug, made by ten-year-old Eli Davenport Hewell (of the Hewell family of famous Georgia potters), were dropped from atop the museum in imitation of the Peach Drop in Atlanta. The miniature jugs rained down and were hastily grabbed by lucky townspeople.

In its heyday, the Bartow County Jail was a hanging jail, and the tower where the jugs were dropped is where the noose would be dropped, with a prisoner attached—but never here. According to records, no prisoner was ever hanged here.

Which brings us to the **Jug Towns** in Georgia that were named for families of potters who used clay, kaolin and fuller's earth deposits that naturally occur in Georgia soils. They went into business making pots, selling their wares to farmers. Durable jugs and crocks were in great demand in the late 1800s for the storage of butter, syrup, buttermilk (it would be set in the chilly water of mountain springs to prevent spoilage), sauerkraut, pickled beans and, most important, moonshine.

These were family businesses, with the next generation serving as apprentices to the older ones. As their pottery operations grew, small shops developed, and so did small towns around the shops. These towns were called

Pottery of the Meaders family on display at the Folk Pottery Museum in Sautee-Nacoochee. *Photo by Robert Gaare.*

Jug Towns, with each Jug Town producing wares uniquely its own. There were five main potter clans: the Meaders, Cravens, Hewells, Dorseys and Fergusons, all now taking their skills into the seventh generation. According to Cheever Meaders, the true patriarch of that family of potters, "We must have been born with clay in our veins." It was hard work from start to finish. "It's not a thing in the world but man-killing work," says third-generation Meaders family potter Lanier Meaders.

The Georgia potters nearly went out of business in the early 1900s with Prohibition, which forced licensed distillers to close down and cut the demand for whiskey jugs (but increasing the demand for illegal moonshine jugs). At the same time, glass and metal containers became more affordable and abundant.

But a few potters shifted their focus away from practical stoneware to making more artistic creations that would bring in a wealthier patronage. The Meaders were particularly known for their face jugs and their wild and creative pottery depicting animals and snakes and grapes. Most were

Signage at the front of the award-winning Folk Pottery Museum in Sautee-Nacoochee. *Photo by Robert Gaare.*

designed by Arie Meaders, Cheever's wife, and by son Lanier, whose work is featured at the Smithsonian Institution. Others, like the Hewell and Craven families, turned to making garden-ware pottery.

A great place to view the history and works of Georgia potters is at the award-winning, stunningly designed Folk Pottery Museum of Sautee-Nacoochee. It's an amazing and unsung gift to Georgia and well worth seeing. (More on Sautee-Nachoochee in chapter 4.)

7

I'VE BEEN WORKING ON THE RAILROAD

Georgia's towns named for railroad engineers, presidents of railroads and railroad incidents are numerous and far-ranging. Many place-names connected with railroads are scattered throughout this book. But a few towns are so connected with the development of the railways in Georgia that they need special mention in their own chapter.

The story of how **Chamblee** (Decatur) was named is unusual not only because of its connection with the railroad but also because it was named for a black railroad worker. The original community of Chamblee petitioned the federal government for a post office using the name *Roswell Junction*. The petition was denied, as it was a name too similar to that of the Roswell Post Office. So, the powers that be chose a different name: Chamblee, after a well-respected railroad worker, Robert Chamblee, who lived in Gainesville but came to the town regularly for his job on the Charlotte to Atlanta line. The line also ran between Gainesville and Chamblee as part of the journey north and south. Chamblee is the only jurisdiction in Georgia to be named for an African American, and that is why an exception was made to include a town named after a man.

Kennesaw (Cobb), originally called **Big Shanty**, was so named because of a cluster of shanties that housed railroad construction workers. Or it could also be a railway crossing shanty, also known as a watchman's or signalman's shanty, giving the crossing gateman a clear view of the train crossing. One shanty was so large it could be seen at the head of a steep incline, and so the town was named Big Shanty.

Another version of the story is that Big Shanty was so named because it was the high point of the railroad between the Chattahoochee and Etowah Rivers. In railroad terms, this was known as the big grade to the shanties. The name was changed to Kennesaw around 1870 to honor an Indian chief of that same name who signed the Treaty of Holston in 1791, ceding land to the white man.

Kennesaw has been called "the great collision of the Civil War and railroad history." At the time of the Civil War, two-thirds of the railroad lines were laid in the North, leaving any stretch of railroad line in the South at a premium. The Northern troops needed to cut off Chattanooga from the railroads to Atlanta, which would trap the Southern troops in Tennessee. This action would also keep reinforcements from Atlanta from coming to their aid.

Atlanta had become the railroad hub of the South (and the future air travel hub), with four major railroad lines using the city as their terminus. All of this leads up to the Great Locomotive Chase in April 1862.

Northern civilian scout and Union spy from Ohio, James J. Andrews, proposed a raid designed to sever the rail connections and telegraph lines between Chattanooga and Atlanta. Twenty-two men were selected, including railroad engineers, to meet in Marietta, Georgia. Disguised in civilian attire, they were able to use a cover story that they were from Kentucky, looking for a Confederate unit in which to enlist. They easily slipped through the Confederate lines. The plan was for Andrews and the engineers to board the train in Marietta and sit in the same car. When the train reached Big Shanty, Andrews and the engineers would take over the locomotive while the passengers and train crew ate their breakfast. Others working with Andrews would uncouple all but three boxcars. This infamous train was called the *General*.

All was proceeding according to plan. The train made its usual breakfast stop at Big Shanty. The passengers and crew disembarked to have breakfast at the Lacy Hotel while Andrews and his men did their work. In the midst of eating his eggs and bacon, the *General*'s conductor, William A. Fuller, saw through the window of the hotel restaurant his train depart, and without him. The *General* was being stolen. Immediately, he began to organize a pursuit.

Desiring not to raise alarm, Andrews and his men maintained the train's schedule, moving at normal speed, occasionally stopping to place a rail/obstacle on the tracks, cut a telegraph line or to stop for wood and water.

In the meantime, Fuller walked at a fast clip, borrowed a horse and obtained a handcar in pursuit of his train. When in Etowah, he commandeered a train called the *Yonah*, traveling north, but he had to wait for the tracks to clear at Kingston. He spotted the *Texas*, going south, stopped it and then boarded and commandeered it. As it was traveling south, he had to continue the chase with the *Texas* going in reverse.

And so the great locomotive chase began. The *Texas* was closing in on the *General*. Thrown railway ties failed to slow down the *Texas*. With the *Texas* nearing and the *General*'s fuel nearly depleted, Andrews directed his men to abandon the train just two miles short of Ringgold, just past Tunnel Hill and fifteen miles from Chattanooga and the Union lines. They scattered into the wilderness. All were captured within a few days and taken to Atlanta. Andrews and seven others were executed, without a real trial. Rebel guards were said to argue over the honor of being the hangmen. Eight others managed to escape and return to the Union lines. The six remaining prisoners were eventually released in a prisoner-of-war exchange.

The *General* now resides at the Southern Locomotive Museum in Kennesaw. The *Texas* resides at the Atlanta History Center, with the newly relocated and restored *Cyclorama* depicting the Battle of Atlanta.

Tunnel Hill (Catoosa) figured in the Great Locomotive Chase but has its own story to tell. The town, first called *Doe Run* and then incorporated as *Tunnelsville*, is named for the tunnel known as the Chetoogeta Mountain Tunnel, a 1,497-foot railroad tunnel built in the late 1840s. The rugged North Georgia Mountains blocked the southern push of the railroads. Chetoogeta Mountain was the most formidable of all, preventing the connection between Atlanta and Chattanooga by rail. Using mostly slave labor, a tunnel had to be dug by the Western and Atlantic Railroad.

Plans began in the late 1830s, but a great panic and depression delayed the construction for almost ten years. Building was restarted in 1848 and completed in 1850. A town came to life in the area, providing services to the needs of the passengers from the train and the "sappers" building the tunnel. A *sapper* is a term for a soldier whose job it is to build and repair roads and bridges and sometimes lay mines.

It was the engineering marvel of its time, completely constructed by hand, and was the first railroad tunnel completed south of the Mason-Dixon line. Limestone blocks were blasted and cut from the surface rock on Rocky Face Ridge. Once freed, these heavy stones were transported using stone boats for the five to six miles to the tunnel construction site, on either the western or eastern end. The tunnel was dug from both sides, with the walls and arches made of stone and brick.

Backside of the tunnel at Tunnel Hill showing how much had to be dug out of Chetoogeta Mountain. *Photo by Robert Gaare.*

The entrance to the 1,497-foot railroad tunnel at Tunnel Hill, where the Great Locomotive Chase ended. *Photo by Robert Gaare.*

A new tunnel has been constructed, parallel to the old one, which has been paved for tourists to walk through and read the historical markers. "Don't be too optimistic," it is said. "The light at the end of the tunnel may be another train!"

During the nearby Battle of Chickamauga, Confederate general John B. Hood was wounded by shrapnel in the right leg. He was brought to the close-

The marker at Tunnel Hill, where General John Bell Hood's leg was supposedly buried after being amputated. *Photo by Robert Gaare.*

by Little Farm, where the doctors amputated the leg in the hopes of saving his life. Later, he was brought to the Clisby-Austin House, used as a hospital, to recuperate. His amputated leg was brought with him. In case the general did not survive the amputation, the powers that be wanted him buried as a whole. When his doctors became convinced he would survive, his rotting leg was buried in Tunnel Hill at the family cemetery of the Clisby-Austin House. A wooden "footstone" was erected over the leg's final resting place and eventually replaced by a granite marker. Local Civil War reenactors have reported seeing the ghost of a one-legged Confederate soldier walking through a nearby field, presumably looking for his missing leg.

The story of the leg being buried at the Clisby-Austin House is a legend, not to be believed by Civil War aficionados. Some say his leg was buried elsewhere, closer to the Chickamauga battlefield. A few more say that Hood lost his leg in the narrow tunnel by carelessly dangling it outside a train. But most say the leg was buried at the Little Farm, where it was amputated. Once the doctors thought General Hood would survive, the leg was put to rest. There's a small plaque at the farm.

8

FROM BEES TO CEMENT TO SILK

GEORGIA'S INDUSTRIAL PLACE-NAMES

This section is by no means intended to be inclusive, just representative of the many towns, both existing and no longer existing, named after Georgia industries.

Hahira (Lowndes) is one of my favorite Georgia place-names. The origin of the name remains a mystery, but there are three stories that attempt to solve it. Folklore says that the name came from the Bible, in Exodus 14:2. The children of Israel camped at Pi-Hahiroth, where the Egyptians overtook them. Some say that town founder Berry J. Folsom named it after a river in Liberia, as Hahira means "good water." (Good luck locating the Hahira River on a map.) More interesting folklore says there was a resident named Hira who would stop by the railroad tracks to rest and watch the "iron horse" go by. When the train passed by, passengers would wave their hands and say, "Hey, Hira!" Some say Hira was a locomotive engineer who was hailed by his friends as he passed through town. Mystery solved?

But why include Hahira in the industrial place-names section? In the late 1920s, a group of Hahira tobacco businessmen decided that, instead of shipping their raw product north, they should manufacture their own brand of cigarettes in Hahira. And they did, producing the O'teen brand (five cents a pack) and then the Happy Days Cigarettes (unconditionally guaranteed to be of superior quality). Hahira was labeled the "Gold Leaf City of the South." But this business eventually died out, and the building was demolished. The beams of the heart pine foundation and flooring were salvaged for future use.

Welcoming sign to Hahira and the Hahira Bee Festival. *Photo by Robert Gaare.*

One of the uses of the beams was in the building of the Puett Company, established for the raising and packaging of queen bees sold all over the United States and Canada. Hahira now became known as the "Queen Bee Capital of the World." With the death of Garnett Puett, a third-generation Puett, the company came to its demise. But Dadant and Sons Inc., the oldest and largest manufacture of beekeeping supplies in the world, bought the Puetts out and opened a branch office and warehouse of their company, based in Hamilton, Illinois. This branch closed in 1996 due to a consolidation of branches in High Springs, Florida. But what lives on is the Hahira Honey Bee Festival, now approaching its fortieth year, held the first week in October. Up to thirty-six thousand visitors have been known to come every year to the festival.

There are a number of Georgia towns named for the stone or mineral industry. **Lithonia** (DeKalb) derives from the Greek word *lithos*, meaning "stone," and *onia*, meaning "place." A classics teacher in the area is responsible for suggesting the coined name. The area contains an abundance of gneiss granite, the best example being the granite dome known as Stone Mountain, the largest exposed piece of granite on earth. One of Georgia's Seven Natural Wonders, the side of the mountain was carved with another "largest"—the largest bas-relief sculpture in the world, featuring three central figures of the Confederacy: Generals Stonewall Jackson and Robert E. Lee, and Jefferson Davis, president of the Confederacy. It took three sculptors and fifty years' time to finish the giant piece. Each summer, picnickers can witness a laser and sound show on the carved side, bringing the figures and other laser projections to life while a recorded Elvis sings "The Battle Hymn of the Republic."

Flintstone (Walker) is not named for the cartoon family but for a nearby source of flintstone, commonly used by the Cherokees who lived there.

Asbestos (White) was the name of a former community named for the fire-resistant material asbestos, which was mined there. Georgia was the first state to mine asbestos commercially. Later, asbestos was proven to be harmful. The EPA and other federal organizations set regulations on asbestos. Since people today spend a lot of money removing asbestos from public and private buildings, it's no wonder the town went bust.

Marble Hill (Pickens) is named for its marble deposits. Georgia is ranked second to Vermont in marble quarries. Marble work began as far back as the days of the Cherokees, but quarrying operations didn't begin until after their removal. In 1884, the Southern Marble Company, or the Southern Marble Quarries, a Massachusetts-based company, began its quarry operation in Georgia in the town of Marble Hill. With the completion of a railroad loop in 1897, the company officially opened for business and is still in operation today.

Cement (Bartow) was a once-flourishing town named for the cement industry. In 1850, Wallace Howard consulted with the chemist St. Julien Ravenel of Charleston concerning the deposit of natural cement rock found in the area. Cement is a fine-grained clay limestone compound that turns into a solid bonding agent when mixed with water. When analyzed, the cement was found to be of high quality. The manufacture of cement began in 1851, as did the naming of the town. Manufacture ceased during the Civil War. Afterward, the company was bought out by Howard's son-in-law. The company's product, Howard Hydraulic Cement, was declared superior to any in the country. It was used to build the East River Bridge in New York City, the Biltmore House in Asheville, the Atlanta Railroad Depot and two bridges across the Tennessee River, to name a few. A demolition contractor in Atlanta lost money on his bid to raze the Fulton County Jail and Atlanta Custom House due to the quality of Howard

Marble slab at the front of the offices of Imerys Operations in Marble Hill. *Photo by Robert Gaare.*

Cement, used in the buildings' foundations. The company went out of business by 1911, when the cement deposit was exhausted.

The Rock (Upson) is not really named for its rock quarries but because the mail train would leave its mailbag on a large rock by the tracks. It was the only safe and dry place available for a central mail drop. The rock had a large cleft on its side, making it possible for the mail to remain there safely until it could be retrieved. The expression "going to the rock to get the mail" originated right here! The rock was eventually blasted by the Georgia Department of Transportation for the highway to go through, but a marker is left to denote the place where the original post office was located.

Mica (Cherokee), **Iron City** (Seminole), **Quartz** (Walker), **Furnace** (Walker), **Jet** (Carroll) and **Aragon** (Polk) were also appropriately named for the minerals mined in these locations.

Lumber has long been a big part of Georgia's resources and products. **Sawdust** (Columbia) housed several sawmills powered by a local creek. **Flatwoods** (Gilmer) was named for the rich stand of hardwoods.

Lumber City (Telfair) was an area of pine forest that had been involved in several litigations over the years. In the late 1800s, a company of Maine lumbermen, seeing great possibilities, bought up large amounts of land and opened several sawmills that failed. They deserted the whole setup, leaving the mills to rot. Land thieves took over, illegally selling the lands to purchasers, who subsequently improved the lots. Big squabbles resulted over who really owned the land. There were acts of violence resulting in imprisonments. The courts took over to resolve the issues. With the railways soon opening up, more lumbermen came in. After the disputes were settled, the land was resold for a pittance. The area became populated by thrifty Scotchmen, who were also involved in the turpentine industry.

Sapps Still (Coffee) was the site of a turpentine still in the early 1900s until the still exploded due to a fire. There are more than fifty uses for turpentine.

A *naval store* is the term used for all products derived from pinesap, such as turpentine, rosin, pitch and tar. Pine tree gum was heated in a large saucer until part of the gum vaporized. The residue was called tar or pitch and was used in sealing ships. The scraping of pine trees killed them, so eventually a new and less harmful way to make turpentine and tar had to be discovered. Pine trees have to be constantly replenished in order to keep up with the demand for the naval stores. Killing them off too soon through scraping quickly cut into your supply and profit.

A typical turpentine distillery. *Library of Congress.*

Eldorado (Tift) was first known as *Fender,* for the Fender Turpentine Works, but it was renamed Eldorado to signify the richness of the naval stores industry. The name mimicked the legend of El Dorado, a Spanish king who was said to be always covered in gold dust and lived in a land paved with gold.

Steam Mill (Seminole) was named for its early steam-operated turpentine distillery.

Some miscellaneous or hard-to-categorize place-names were too interesting to leave out. Miscellaneous industry-named towns include **Cairo** (Grady), pronounced "kay row," a leading producer of cane sugar. Cairo produces more sugar syrup than anywhere in the world during the fall months.

Pabst (Houston) was the site of a southeastern site for the Pabst Brewing Company, now closed.

Experiment (Spalding) is so named for the Georgia Agricultural Experiment Station, established by University of Georgia–Athens to conduct horticulture experiments.

The modern mechanism attached to a truck for easier removal of pecans. *Library of Congress.*

Pecan City (Dougherty) is named for its pecan crop. Due to improved soil conditions and research by the experiment stations, annual production of pecans in Georgia has doubled since 1935. This is due to the development of the tree shaker, an eccentric and piston-driven device attached to the tree by a cable, which, when set in motion, causes the shaking of the tree. The result is a showering of pecans. Pecan trees are not very obliging about dropping their pecans, even in a stiff wind. This machine replaced the old-fashioned method of children climbing the limbs of a pecan tree to shake them while their parents, down below, gathered the nuts.

Thunder (Upson) was named for the Creek warrior Big Thunder and refers to the rumbling noise, like thunder, caused by natural gas escaping from the earth, and not from him!

Scienceville (Scudder) was named by a local science teacher who wanted to stress the study of pure sciences in public schools. This was in the pre-STEM (science, technology and math) era.

Industry (Fulton) was built in proximity to railroad junctions and named for the industrial future it promised.

Flexatile (Bartow) was an old mining settlement. Slabs of slate were quarried here, sawed into proper sizes and marketed as slate shingles.

Richardson Company of Lockland, Ohio, purchased the property in 1920 through its subsidiary, Flexatile, the name given to the community surrounding the plant. It explored the coloring of slate tiles and crushed the slate, to be used as mineral filler in fertilizer. In 1927, Funkhouser Company of Hagerstown, Maryland, purchased the plant and made green-colored composition roofing materials. The name then changed to *Funkhouser*. Mining ceased in the early 1960s.

Tax (Talbot) was so named because county tax officials stopped here to receive tax returns.

What about the silk towns of **Ebenezer**, **Silk Hope** and **Canton**? When James Oglethorpe settled Georgia in the early 1700s, it was thought that the silk industry would thrive here. With cheap labor and land, trustees from England were sent to Italy for silkworm eggs and brought instructors to teach the colonists in the production of silk. There were covenants requiring a sufficient number of white mulberry trees standing on every acre to promote the silk culture.

The silk industry began to thrive, especially with the Salzberger settlement in **Ebenezer** (see more in chapter 11). Queen Caroline of England appeared in 1735 in a full robe made from Georgia silk, declaring it to be as fine as any Italian silk. But labor was so poorly paid, even with the use of slave labor, that the silk culture diminished. During the Revolutionary War, the British took over Ebenezer, putting an end to its silk production. After the war, the cultivation of rice and cotton in the area proved to be more profitable.

Silk Hope (Chatham) was one of the first Georgia colony towns hoping to establish a flourishing silk industry.

Canton (Cherokee), previously known as *Etowah*, also tried to establish a silk industry. Located on the opposite side of the state from Silk Hope, 100,000 silkworms were imported there. The name of the town was changed to Canton, named after China's great silk center. Two prominent settlers, William Grisham and Joseph Donaldson (the grandfather of golfer Bobby Jones), had dreams of making Canton the center of the silk industry in the United States.

Canton never became a significant silk center but, rather, a successful manufacturing center and mill town, producing "Canton Denim," known the world over until the Canton Cotton Mills closed in 1981.

To close with a bit of humor, **Split Silk** (Walton) is not named for its silk industry. It was reportedly given this name when a girl accidentally tore her silk dress in front of the C.L. Ivey General Store. (More in chapter 19.)

9

FROM HARDSCRABBLE TO GOOD HOPE

Georgia has a number of po'mouth names for old, mostly nonexistent, Georgia towns. What's a po'mouth name? It's a bad-mouthin' name that comes from the townspeople themselves who are making fun of the desperate nature of their town, usually a rural, isolated farming community. The term comes from within the town and townspeople, and does not refer to names applied by people on the outside.

Cracker's Neck (Greene) was a place-name applied by outsiders commenting on the "crackers" in the town who were having a hard time making a living. The term *Georgia Crackers* refers to the original American pioneer settlers who came to Georgia in the 1700s. Now the term is widely used as an ethnic slur for white people who live in poor rural sections of the American South.

Buttermilk Bottoms (Fulton) was a po'mouth name given by the residents themselves, who had to depend on buttermilk, an inexpensive drink and readily available as long as you had cows and a nearby creek to serve as a refrigerator. Other po'mouth examples are **Hard Fortune** (McDuffie) and **Pull Tight** (Decatur). Both names refer to residents having to pull tight their belts in order to survive.

There are many more po'mouth names. Here are a few more I found.

Scourgetown Community (Gilmer) either meant a place where people crowded too close together or had a scourge of a time making a living.

Hardscrabble (Fulton) implied it was hard to make a living there.

Hardup (Webster) was so named because early merchants were stingy and greedy, making it "hard" for residents to come "up" with money to buy anything.

And we can't forget **Useless Bay** (Clinch), so named because the natives proclaimed, "Hit's hard to get about in and ain't fit fer nuthin."

Then there are the "always hungry" po'mouthin' towns like **Rabbit Hill** (Bryan), where residents had to rely on rabbit meat in order to get by. **Lickskillet** (Harris) residents named the former community after a man who so enjoyed his fish fry meal that he offered to "lick the skillet" clean.

Hungry Hill (Bryan) is actually not a hill but is as flat as can be. Perhaps it got its name from surveyors mapping out lots for the Georgia land lottery who ran out of provisions while working there. They went hungry, so the name stuck.

Communities with optimistic titles are often next door to the po'mouthin' ones. For example, **Providence** and **Hopewell** sit next to **Hardscrabble**.

This brings us to the opposite, "be of good cheer" town names, starting with **Providence** (Fulton), which is next to the po'mouth community of Hardscrabble, so named to denote optimism as opposed to down-and-out bad luck. There was a community of the same name in Sumter County. Both had prominent churches with the same name.

Ideal (Macon) is another example. Before the railway came through, Ideal was *Joetown*. But when two railroad executives were looking for a place to stop, they arrived there, and one man said the site was "ideal." The other man said, "You have just named it!"

Benevolence (Randolph), settled in 1831, was so named when founder Thomas

Road sign approaching Hopeulikit with blue skies ahead. *Photo by Robert Gaare.*

Coram gave five acres to the Baptist Church and Cemetery, a benevolent deed indeed that supplied the new name of the town.

In **Plentitude** (Jones), many settlers moved on, but many stayed, as there was plenty here and in abundance.

Unincorporated **Amity** (Lincoln) was a town name meaning "harmony" and "friendliness."

Jolly (Pike) was formerly called *Traveler's Rest* because it was a convenient and convivial rest stop for early wagon train drivers. When the railroad came through, a railroad worker suggested the town be called Jolly, as its residents (as in Amity) were full of good humor.

The same could be said about **Gay** (Meriwether). Alas, it was named for W.F. Gay, the first mayor and first store owner and the grandson of the real founder, William Sasser. The town couldn't be named for Sasser, as the name had already been taken.

Good Hope (Walton) was named for the settlers' good hopes for this community. Good Hope is still around, with a population of 210 in the 2000 Census.

There are plenty of other hopeful towns in Georgia, including **Hopewell** (Camden and Fulton) and **Hopeful** (Mitchell). A sign hangs over the Hopeful General Store: "Life is simple. Eat, sleep, and fish." **Hopeulikit** (Bulloch) is featured in chapter 19.

Welcome (Coweta) was named by J.B. Hutchens after his friend, Welcome Carter, one of the original settlers. But others in the know think the town gained its name for the friendly Indians who made the early settlers feel welcome.

Sunnyside (Spalding) and **Sunbury** (Liberty) were both so named because of their sunny southern exposures.

Tarrytown (Montgomery) was thus called, not after a city in New York or elsewhere, but because it was an ideal place to tarry.

Folkston (Charlton) was named in honor of Dr William Brandon Folks, a prominent physician and surgeon to all the folks nearby. Folkston is the self-proclaimed "Marriage Capital of the World." Floridians living just over the border, who could not endure their state's waiting period before getting hitched, crossed the Georgia state line to wed. Folkston folks were eager to receive them.

Although I've made it a point not to include many towns named after men, **Fitzgerald** is one of the exceptions. Fitzgerald (Ben Hill) might be Georgia's city of brotherly love. After the Civil War, an Indiana newspaper publisher, Philander H. Fitzgerald, who was once a drummer boy for the Union army, assembled a group of Union vets who were tired of the northern winters.

Photo of a Confederate war veteran and a Union war veteran shaking hands, representative of the spirit of Fitzgerald. *Library of Congress.*

They wanted to move south. But what was the draw for them to move into former enemy territory?

There was a drought in the Midwest in 1894. Georgia governor William J. Northen, eager to populate some of the sparse areas of the wiregrass region of the Georgia coast, organized a relief committee that shipped flour, corn and meat for free distribution into the former enemy territory, now suffering from shortages due to the drought.

This friendly gesture appealed to Philander and other Union vets. They came south to Fitzgerald and purchased fifty thousand acres of forest land to start the American Soldiers Colony Association, composed of Union veterans. Whole families came in prairie schooners, bringing their children, furniture and pets, living in shacks until a city could be built. They sang old camp songs at night like "Marching through Georgia." Now they were marching *to* Georgia.

This seemed a very strange concept: so many northerners interested in settling in the Deep South not long after the end of the Civil War. But this "Colony City," later named Fitzgerald after Philander, appealed to the locals. There was little strife among the new colonists and old residents. Looking for unity, city streets were named equally after Union and Confederate generals.

A memorial hotel was built and called the Lee-Grant Hotel. A Blue-Gray Museum opened in the 1970s to tell the story of how blue and gray veterans created Georgia's "City of Harmony." Beth Davis, a descendant of a Union soldier who moved to the area, started the museum with her husband. It was first located in their laundromat and then moved into the old depot.

Fitzgerald, ironically, is close to Irwinville, Georgia, where Jefferson Davis, president of the Confederacy, was captured. (More on that story in chapter 5.)

10

COINAGE

A coined name is an original name created by combining words, parts of words or letters. Or it can be created by altering spelling, by matching syllable sounds or by inventing a new word entirely. This chapter features some examples of Georgia coined names, from Trion to Adel to Ty Ty.

A flip of the coin, and first up is **Trion** (Walker), named for a trio of Lafayette businessmen. Judge A.P. Allgood, Judge Spence Marsh and Colonel W.K. Byars settled in this new town in 1847. In order to commemorate their partnership, the Trion Mills cotton mill was established that same year. It managed to escape Federal destruction by General William Tecumseh Sherman some twenty years later. Supposedly, Sherman spent the night at A.P. Allgood's house and, the next morning, out of gratitude and friendship, gave protection papers to the town and mill. A large guard was sent to protect the mill property, with Sherman's men destroying and scavenging all around the mill, but for food only. The mill stopped running after the Federal invasion until peace was declared in 1865.

After the war, Allgood was not a popular person. Arsonists burned the mill to the ground in 1875, possibly because of his Unionist stance, but the person or persons who started the fire and the why and wherefore remain unknown. Today, the mills are called the Mount Vernon Mill No. 3, whose products have made Trion the "Denim Capital of the World." (See also **Canton** in chapter 8.)

Smoky Row was a section of Trion that was named during a typhoid epidemic. People were told that if they burned logs in the street and created a great deal of smoke, it would help them avoid contracting the disease. People didn't realize that mosquitoes caused the disease; it was the smoke that drove the mosquitoes away.

Redan (DeKalb) was a coined name taken from original settlers N.M. Reid and Annie Alford, making Reid Ann, which was reduced to Redan.

Subligna (Chattooga) was a community named for one of its founders, Dr. William Dunlap Underwood. But the place-name *Underwood* had already been taken, so the town's Latin teacher coined a new word based on the Latin words *sub* ("under") and *ligna* ("wood"). The town still managed to honor Dr. Underwood by using the Latin version of his name.

Luxomni (Gwinnett) was also a coined name from two Latin words: *lux* for "light" and *omni* for "all." Luxomni was a flag station erected near Lilburn by the Seaboard Air Line Railroad in 1891, and it needed a name. Often, towns are named for prominent citizens. But not this one. A civil engineer who worked for the railroad suggested the Latin coined name *Luxomni*, meaning "light for all."

Dacula (Gwinnett) is an early rail town named by using certain letters in Decatur and Atlanta, coined to make the unusual name of Dacula, pronounced "day coo la."

Clem (Carroll) was originally named for the Coleman brothers, Jim and Allen, who had a gristmill and a gin on Whooping Creek. They were prominent in the community, and it was suggested the depot and town be named for them. However, there was already a Coleman, Georgia. So, the first conductor at the depot picked four letters from the brothers' last name: C, L, E and M. In this way, the town's name was born.

Tyus (Carroll) was so named because Andrew Hallum and Jack Tyus tossed a coin for whose name would be the basis for the town's name. Jack Tyus won, hence the town was named for him.

Ocee (Fulton) is situated on an elevation. When the land was farmed and the air was clear enough to see the horizon in all directions, someone might exclaim, "Oh, see!" And they did and so named the town.

Adel (Cook) was first named *Puddleville*. Pioneer settler Joel J. "Uncle Jack" Parrish, the first postmaster, didn't like the name. To create the new name, he took the middle four letters of the name *Philadelphia*, which he saw on a crocus sack, to come up with Adel.

Adel is now the Cook County seat. A lime sink is located here. It is said that the bottom has never been reached and never goes dry. At one time it served as a baptismal pool for the adjacent Salem Primitive Baptist Church, built in 1859. It now serves as a fishing hole for area residents.

There are numerous lime sinks in South Georgia. Simply put, a lime sink is a sinkhole found in limestone areas of the state. Water trickles down through the limestone over a period of thousands of years, creating underground caves that eventually collapse, forming these deep holes.

Sparks (Cook) was originally named *Afton*. Although the new town name honors a Mr. Sparks, who was the railroad division president (yes, another railroad president who had the town named after him), I include Sparks, following the inclusion of Adel, because of a saying that sprang up: "Adel is so close to Hell you can see Sparks."

There are a few place-names that are simply fun to say. **Ty Ty** (Tift) is one of them. The name refers to dense ty ty thickets, similar to wax myrtles, that can grow to over thirty feet in height and that bloom in late spring and early summer. Georgia surveyors applied the name *Tight Eye* to creeks; the name *Ty Ty* could have been a derivation. But more than likely, the name Ty Ty was suggested because of the many heartland railroad ties that were cut and sold in this community.

There was a Lulu Bobo, who was a town correspondent at one time. Local people loved to say "Lulu Bobo from Ty Ty"—three repeating syllables in a row: lu, bo and ty. There are only three known towns in the United States with repeating syllable names with spaces between the repetitions: Ty Ty, Georgia; Paw Paw, Michigan; and Walla Walla, Washington.

11

IT SAYS SO IN THE BIBLE

Not surprisingly, there are many place-names in Georgia with religious or biblical origins. This chapter will highlight some of them.

Ai (Gilmer) was a place mentioned in the Bible thirty-two times in the book of Joshua. Ai was one of the royal cities of the Canaanites, where Joshua suffered a defeat, then a victory. The word generally means "ruins."

Mars Hill (Cobb) was the hill named for the Roman god of war, Mars, and the Greek god Ares. It was on this hill that Mars/Ares was tried by the gods for the murder of Poseidon's son. Mars Hill remained an important meeting place, where philosophy, religion and law were discussed.

It was also where the Apostle Paul spoke to the idolatrous Athenians. Paul traveled with Silas and Timothy to Athens, a city of about 250,000 people, including slaves. Once the center of the Greek empire, Mars Hill had become a part of the Roman Empire. There were many temples, altars, idols and statues in the city. To the Jewish teacher Paul, those idols spoke to a false god or gods. He was there to spread the news of the Messiah, which he did loudly and clearly in one of his most important gospel sermons.

Abel (Peach) comes from the name of Adam and Eve's second son, Abel, the keeper of the flock. Cain, being the first son, was angry at Abel over offerings they both made to God. Abel's gift was accepted, but Cain's was not, as it was given "with a wrong attitude of heart." He was given a second chance to make it right, but his anger and jealousy overcame him. He murdered his brother. Abel is thought of as the first man to be martyred for his faith and the first shepherd of the Bible.

Hephzibah (Richmond) was originally named *Brothersville* to honor three of its initial settlers, the Anderson brothers: James, Augustus and Elisha Jr. They built the first homes in the area. The name was changed to Hephzibah, from the book of Second Kings in the Bible. The name is a symbol for Zion and is said to mean "my delight is in her." Hephzibah was King Hezekiah's wife. Also known as Hafzbah, the name also means "guarding" or "taking care of," suggesting the idea of safekeeping. Hephzibah denotes someone who evokes delight, but also one who is protected by God's favor. The name might have been originally taken from the Hephzibah Baptist Association, which established a denominational high school there in 1860.

Newborn (Newton) was originally known as *Crossroads* or *Sandtown*. Methodist evangelist Sam P. Jones preached stirring sermons to the community. He wanted the inhabitants to feel as if they were "born anew" after hearing him preach. Thus, the name of the town was changed to Newborn.

Goshen (Chatham) was an old German/Moravian settlement near the Georgia coast. The name was derived from the part of Egypt called the "Land of Goshen," where the Israelites settled. The sons of Jacob experienced a severe famine that lasted seven years. Word was out that Egypt was the only kingdom able to supply food, so the sons journeyed there to buy goods. In the second year of famine, the pharaoh invited them to live in the country of Goshen, described as the best land in Egypt, suitable for both crops and livestock. After the death of Joseph, the Egyptians feared potential integration of Israelites into their population or a takeover, so they enslaved the Israelites and took away their rights. Moses came 430 years later and led the Israelites out of Egypt. The term *Land of Goshen* has always referred to a land rich and fruitful.

Smyrna (Cobb) is today known as the "Jonquil City." After completion of the Western and Atlantic Railroad in 1842, the area was named *Varner's Station*, *Ruff's Siding*, *Neal Dow* and *Ruff's Station*. A religious encampment called Smyrna Camp Ground became a popular destination. Was the city of Smyrna named after the campground? Or was it more than likely named after the ancient seaport of Asia Minor, the birthplace of Homer? It was also the name of the second of the seven churches mentioned in the Book of Revelation. In a nod to ancient Greece, Smyrna, Georgia, has Greek-inspired architecture in the look of the City Hall Complex.

Since we mentioned the Greek poet, I'd like to include the Georgia town of **Homer**, which, for fifty years, has run what was at one time the world's largest Easter egg hunt, held on Easter Sunday and said to rival any major sporting event. Every year, 100,000 cellophane-wrapped candy eggs are

Early Easter egg hunt at the White House. *Harris & Ewing Collection, Library of Congress.*

scattered over Mack Garrison's ten-acre horse pasture, with 125 of those eggs containing a special surprise. You might win a coupon to be traded in for a live bunny or an Easter basket filled with chocolate marshmallow goodies and a stuffed bunny. Twenty-one years ago, the contest set the coveted Guinness World Record for world's largest Easter egg hunt. The record has been broken many times since, with a number of other towns winning the competition. But Homer is a town of only 950 people, so its recognition was the most special.

Easter egg hunts have been around for a long time, starting as an annual ritual in ancient Europe. Hunters searched woods for the nests of wild birds so they could remove their eggs as the purpose for a hunt. Eventually, the eggs were painted. Woven, plastic and fabric baskets replaced the birds' nests. Today, more plastic eggs are hidden than real, colored, hard-boiled eggs. But the ritual is just as much fun. Every year, the White House hosts an Easter egg hunt and an Easter egg roll on the lawn.

By the way, the town was not named for the Greek poet but for Homer Jackson, an early pioneer. It's unknown if he was named to honor the poet.

Unity (Franklin) was an early church settlement. The town name was based on Ephesians 4:3: "Endeavoring to keep the unity of the spirit in the bond of peace."

Recovery (Decatur) was established during the First Seminole War as a hospital base for soldiers from Fort Scott. Here they would recover from their battle wounds. It was also a hospital during the War of 1812 and the Civil War. Along with great care, prayers and good wishes were used to help the recovery of the soldiers.

Ephesus (Heard) was named after the ancient city in Turkey and was another one of the seven churches of Asia cited in the Book of Revelation. The Gospel of John may have been written there. A legend says that Mary, mother of Jesus, may have spent the last years of her life here after his crucifixion. It is a popular place for Catholic pilgrimages.

Patmos (Baker) is a hamlet named after the Isle of Patmos in the Bible. John, beloved disciple of Jesus, was banished to Patmos during the later years of his life. Patmos was a small, rocky, barren area where many criminals from Rome were sent to serve out their prison sentences. John was sent there for being a troublemaker and a member of a cult. Conditions there were harsh. Prisoners were forced to work in the mines. After arriving, John began to have visions from Jesus that were described in the Book of Revelation, the last book of the Christian Bible. Some scholars think that John died on this island.

Temperance (Telfair) was named for a citizen, Temperance Griffin, not because of the temperance movement against the use and sale of alcohol, although the name seems fitting. There is a large Methodist campground here.

Zoar (Bulloch) was the city that Lot and his daughters fled to from Sodom. While the sinful places of Sodom and Gomorrah were destroyed by "fire and brimstone," Zoar was not, leaving it a refuge for Lot and his family.

Archery (Webster) is the place where former president Jimmy Carter was born, which makes it noteworthy for that reason alone. This rural community had a history before becoming known as the boyhood farm of our thirty-ninth president. The St. Mark African Methodist Episcopal (AME) Church and school for black youth were unique to the area and the times. The community itself was named for the Sublime Order of Archery, a relief organization of the AME Church that assisted southern black families. Two white families lived there, one being the Carters, in addition to the twenty-five black families. The school, opened by Bishop William Decker Johnson, operated for the sole purpose of providing education and resources to black youth. Male and female students received education from primary to college level and also received vocational training.

Near Archery is **Plains** (Sumter). Jimmy Carter went to school here, and he announced his campaign for the presidency at the Plains Depot. The town was once known as the Plain of Dura, after the province in

Author's uncle, Al Kaemmerlen, poking his head out of the giant cutout peanut in downtown Plains, home of Jimmy and Rosalynn Carter. *Photo by Robert Gaare.*

Babylon established by King Nebuchadnezzar, who made a colossal image of gold and set it upon the plain. According to the third chapter of the Book of Daniel, Nebuchadnezzar then commanded everyone to bow down to his image. Shadrach, Meshach and Abednego refused and were thrown into a hot furnace, but the fires did not consume them. The miracle impressed Nebuchadnezzar, who gave them jobs with him and then mended his ways.

Plains, Georgia, which always used the plural form—the name shortened from Plain of Dura to Plains—is situated in one of the state's most lucrative farming regions. There are pine trees, peanut fields, soybeans, magnolias and the ever-pestilent gnat.

Plains was a boomtown of the 1920s. The Wise Sanitarium was located there. The hospital was staffed with some of the most renowned physicians in the South. Lillian Carter, Jimmy's mother, was a nurse there, and Jimmy was born in this hospital. People came from all over to be treated by the Wise brothers and Dr. J.C. Logan.

Plains had one of the finest schools in the area, run by Superintendent Julia L. Coleman, who taught both Jimmy and Rosalynn Carter. She instilled in her students the virtues of human kindness, something the Carters are known for today, with the Carter Center and the Rosalynn Carter Institute of Caregiving. Ms. Coleman told Jimmy he had the ability to be anything he wanted (including becoming the thirty-ninth president of the United States).

Nearby **Koinonia Farms** (Sumter), pronounced "coy no nee a," is a Christian commune founded in 1942 with 440 acres and an early population of only four people. The name came from the original Greek version of the New Testament, meaning a fellowship or community. Today, it encompasses 1,500 acres with a population of eighty people. Clarence and Florence Jordan and Martin and Mabel England were the founders, establishing a set of social precepts that differed from southern social codes of the time. Communal living, an open attitude of racial reconciliation and a philosophy of nonviolence made the members and the farm the target of racial violence. Today, it is best known for its role in the creation of Habitat for Humanity, headquartered in nearby Americus (featured in chapter 17). Tours are available upon request.

Ebenezer (Effingham) (also mentioned in chapter 8) is perhaps the largest, oldest and most interesting religious-based Georgia town. Ebenezer was established in 1734 as a religious refuge for 150 Salzburger emigrants brought over with the consent of James Oglethorpe, founder of Georgia and its first governor. These Protestant refugees had been expelled by the Catholic archbishop of Salzburg in present-day Austria. They were initially sent to Augsburg, Germany, persecuted as Lutherans and forced to flee Germany for the colony of Georgia.

The trustees of the colony of Georgia invited the persecuted Salzburgers to come to the thirteenth colony, paying their way and allotting each family fifty acres of land, providing for them until the first crop could be harvested. Pleased to be there, the residents named their town Ebenezer, which is Hebrew for "stone of help."

They first settled in the old town of Ebenezer, but after they lost a child from the bite of a big rattlesnake while clearing brush, they left. They felt it too dangerous a place to live, so they fled to the coast, which was a better location with more access to trade and supplies.

The soil in the first location proved to be unproductive; the settlers flourished, however, in the new location, located near the Savannah River. The town grew rapidly, and they began many silk mills. Beginning in 1736, each Salzburger was presented with a mulberry tree and instructions in the

Jerusalem Lutheran Church, Georgia's oldest building still in use and built by the Salzburgers in 1736. *Photo by Robert Gaare.*

Statue of Johann Martin Boltzius, an early pastor of the Ebenezer Lutheran Church, who wanted to establish an utopian community there. *Photo by Robert Gaare.*

art of reeling. By 1749, over seven hundred pounds of cocoons yielded fifty pounds of spun silk.

Using locally produced bricks, they constructed their church, which is still standing and is Georgia's oldest building still in use for its original purpose. Its lofty peak of a steeple is topped with a swan weather vane, one of Martin Luther's favorite symbols for the church. But why a swan?

Jan Hus, whose name meant "goose," died in 1415 and was an important religious figure of the time. His teachings strongly influenced Martin Luther and the Reformation. He was excommunicated and burned at the stake at the age of forty-five. Just prior to being burned, he refused to recant his beliefs and made this statement, "You are now going to burn a goose, but in a century you will have a swan which you can neither roast nor boil." Martin Luther, the future leader of the Lutheran Church, was considered to be that swan in the prophecy. Thus, the swan became an important symbol to the Salzburgers and other Lutherans, who placed swan weather vanes and plaques atop their homes and barns and on their front porches.

Led by pastor Johann Martin Boltzius, the people of Ebenezer attempted to build a religious utopia on the Georgia frontier. Boltzius wanted to avoid slavery and the plantation agriculture system. They invited other religious refugees into their community, such as the Moravians. The ban on slavery in Georgia was lifted in 1750, isolating the settlement, which continued to resist using slave labor. They found they could not compete and were forced to allow slavery.

Elsewhere in Georgia, the silk culture did not thrive, but it continued in Ebenezer until the Revolutionary War. The British took over the town, interrupting the silk production. The occupation left the town in ruins. The church and town were ransacked. The town was never revived, but the church still stands, surviving Sherman's March to the Sea in 1864 and an 1886 earthquake.

Today, Ebenezer is a ghost town but operates as a very popular religious retreat center.

12

BAD HOMBRES, NOTORIOUS TOWNS, BOOGERY AND...FAIRYLANDS

Georgia has had its fair share of bad dudes, bad towns, hideaways, haunted sightings and…fairytale lands.

This chapter begins with the bad-seed town of **Burnt Fort** (Charlton). Some say it was named for a family named Fort whose home burned, but most say it was named for an old fort destroyed by fire in the early 1800s. In either case, fire was involved. It's a fact that settlers often had to flee from this locale due to Indian uprisings. But what's the real story?

The story actually begins years before the American Revolutionary War, when England and Spain were disputing land rights in the colonies. In order to avoid a territorial war, South Georgia was considered "off limits" by both Great Britain and Spain.

In 1775, Edmond Gray from Virginia started the community now called *New Hanover* in an area that was not part of either Spain or Great Britain. The governor of Georgia offered to let Gray and his band stay and trade with the natives. They were purported to do more than that, furnishing the Indians with plenty of rum. That stirred up lots of trouble in the area. Spain was angered by this and claimed it was a clear violation of territory considered "neutral." They sent a company of soldiers to order Gray out.

Gray and his men entertained the Spanish soldiers. Because they could not read Spanish, Gray and his men claimed they knew nothing of the orders to leave. The Spanish soldiers returned to St. Augustine saying they had fulfilled their duty and thought Gray's band was going to leave. But of course, they did not.

Georgia and South Carolina representatives then came to New Hanover and gave Gray an order to leave the premises in twenty-eight days. Gray was going to leave anyway, as he had been given an offer by Spain to start a trading settlement farther south on the St. Mary's River. Others of his band stayed. After twenty-eight days, the Georgia and South Carolina representatives came back and burned down the town. New Hanover may have disappeared, but the settlers did not. New Hanover became the town of Burnt Fort, which eventually became part of the British colonies.

Trader's Hill (Charlton), also originally claimed by Spain, was a pioneer trading post known for its well-stocked supply of liquor. The Georgia pioneer was at times a hard-drinking, fighting individual who partook in drunken brawls usually involving fists as weapons.

The area was also known as **Fort Alert**, maintained to protect settlers from Indians on the warpath. As the threat of Indian attack subsided with the removal of area Indians in the mid-1800s, the town became the county seat and flourished.

But the drunken brawls continued and kept the Charlton County Jail quite occupied. It was said that once a man was locked up, he stayed locked up. Each prisoner went down a ladder to his cell. The ladder was then withdrawn and the cell padlocked from the outside. Knowing of the lockup situation, guilty prisoners on their way to the jail would make a mad dash for the river before it was too late. If the prisoner outran the sheriff, he would swim across the St Mary's River to Florida, where he would remain in banishment. In these cases, the prisoner was reported as having "gone south."

Trickum (Walker) was originally called *Graysville* after a store owner/saloonkeeper named Gray, who allegedly "tricked" and swindled his customers. It was once said he swindled a drunk out of twenty dollars, a fortune in that day. There are several other towns named Trickum in Georgia.

The town of **Ranger** (Gordon) is named either after a town in North Carolina or for a group of rangers / citizen vigilantes who moved in to take charge of the Cherokee removal in the area. In the 1830s, Georgia nullified the existence of the Cherokee Nation. These self-appointed citizen deputies were said to be so obnoxious in their treatment of the natives that the state and federal militia were forced to disband them.

The area around Tenth Street, commonly known as Mid-Town in Atlanta, was once called **Tight Squeeze** (Fulton). After the Civil War, the city went through a desperate time, with many people being penniless, homeless and jobless. A ragtag group of freedmen and Confederate veterans, who were also morphine addicts, formed the small shantytown called Tight Squeeze. Here, the road curved to avoid a deep ravine, making it a tight squeeze to navigate. Travelers had to slow down to make it through, making them vulnerable to robbers and highwaymen who sometimes murdered passing merchants. John Plaster, who was delivering firewood to customers in Atlanta, was one such victim. It was said that the area was so dangerous it "took a mighty tight squeeze to get through with one's life." A man named Rough Rice tried to publish a newspaper there, but he became disgusted with the lack of sales and opened a liquor establishment instead. He said whiskey sold better than literature.

In 1872, the name was changed to *Blooming Hill* for the elegant single-family homes that sprang up, making this a "considerable little town," according to the *Atlanta Constitution*. In the decades following, this became Atlanta's first urban renewal project, complete with ritzy, expensive shops to attract customers from affluent Atlanta neighborhoods. But with the opening of Lenox Square in 1959, those same customers moved on to the newest concept in shopping—a shopping center, where "you can find everything."

By the 1960s, the area grew more bohemian and was renamed "The Strip," with Atlanta's hippies opening coffee shops and other establishments. The *Great Speckled Bird* went to print as the first Atlanta-based alternative newspaper, confronting issues such as the Vietnam War, racism and injustice. But after the *Bird* stopped publication in 1976, the neighborhood began to harden again, with strip clubs and drugs and prostitutes moving in. Many businesses were set on fire or torn down.

But not for long. Changing once again for the better, this chameleon area is now known as "the most valuable piece of developable land in the South" and is filled with luxury hotels and expensive bars.

Wildwood (Dade) lies close to the Tennessee line and is nestled in a valley between Sand and Lookout Mountains. In Georgia's early pioneer days, it was said that entering the pass into the valley was a sure invitation to be robbed and probably killed.

Pine Log (Bartow) was mentioned in chapter 4. According to the Bartow County Heritage Society's compilation of stories about the county, this area and **Sugar Hill** were once where Bartow County sent its misfits.

Nearby **Hanging Mountain** was where misbehaving convicts were hanged at the summit as an example to others. The side of the mountain has a steep, almost vertical grade; convicts were made to climb it as a punishment and then were hanged at the top. The number of convicts who died there under suspicious circumstances is unknown.

The most notorious of all—place or person—was Blackbeard the pirate. He belongs in this book and chapter, because **Blackbeard Island** (McIntosh) is part of the Georgia Golden Isles and is named for him. Today, Blackbeard Island is part of the U.S. Fish and Wildlife Services and is a sanctuary for fowl, deer, quail, turkey and virgin

Blackbeard's head on the end of the bowsprit, by Charles Ellms. *Engraving from* Pirates Own Book *by Charles Ellms.*

forests. But in the early 1700s, it provided a perfect sanctuary for pirates like Blackbeard, who robbed Spain's galleons of their cargoes of gold and silver. Then he brought his ill-gotten goods to his favorite haunt: Blackbeard Island.

Edward Teach by birth, Blackbeard, a pirate by profession, was known for his long, black hair, his braided beard, pistols and knives in his sash, cutlass in his hand and dagger in his teeth. He attacked ships up and down the East Coast in his ship, the *Queen Anne's Revenge.* He would attack and conquer any vessel in his path.

He claimed to be the brother of the Devil and that only he and the Devil knew where he buried his treasure. The agreement between the two was that the one who lived longer would be the one to have it. The Devil must have won, because Blackbeard was killed in 1718 off the coast of North Carolina by Lieutenant Robert Maynard, who decapitated him and then displayed his head on a pole to serve as a warning to others. Legend says Blackbeard's skull was later ornamented with silver and made into a punch bowl. It is still said to be in existence. There have been many differing reports of skull punch bowl sightings and even a drink or two taken from the bowl.

Blackbeard Island is a favorite digging spot for tourists, who call it Money-Old Fields. They come searching for buried treasure. But nothing has turned up. In 1800, the United States acquired the island for cutting timber for shipbuilding. It later served as a quarantine spot for yellow

Engraving of Edward Teach, known as Blackbeard the Pirate. Engraving by B. Cole. *Library of Congress.*

fever victims. A brick crematory oven for the victims of the fever can be seen on the island.

In 1914, President Woodrow Wilson turned Blackbeard Island into a wildlife preserve. Sea turtles come out at night to lay their eggs on the waterline, leaving the eggs to hatch in the warm sun.

Speaking of the Devil, there are many towns in Georgia with the name Hell attached to them. **Cow Hell** (Laurens) is named for the treacherous bogs that trap cattle in what might be called a bovine Hades.

Hell's Half Acre (Burke) is actually larger than half an acre. It boasts thickets so thick that a hunting dog can't get through.

Devil's Half Acre (Putnam) dates back to the early 1800s, when a man purchased a half acre of land to establish a dram shop, which is another name for a store or tavern where alcoholic beverages are sold. His shop became the site of so much vice that the town was named Devil's Half Acre. After a religious revival in the late 1820s, the town turned moral and dropped the "Devil" term and sinful habits and became Half Acre.

Where did all these notorious bad hombres escape to in order to hide from their pursuers? They may have gone to **Lost Mountain** (Cobb), where Indians would flee after taking livestock or other items from the white men. The "taken" merchandise was considered lost, beyond recovery.

Or they might escape to **Hush Your Mouth Island** (Camden), home to smugglers or other deviants trying to stay out of the public eye. The motto here was "Keep your mouth shut and don't tell."

Or they might escape to **Race Pond** (Charlton). In 1836, U.S. soldiers were stationed there for the purpose of capturing as many Indians as possible and sending them on their way to the Oklahoma Territory. Seminole Indians retreated to the almost impenetrable Okefenokee Swamp and its small islands. Soldiers waited on the outskirts, on Race Pond, for the Indians to sneak off the islands. The story goes that since they had a great deal of leisure time, as the Seminoles were none too eager to get caught, they would while away their free time by constructing a race track. The soldiers would mount their saddle horses and race them. The track is plainly visible today. As for the Seminoles, the soldiers finally penetrated the swamp and drove them out. But many Seminoles found their way to another swamp hideout: the Florida Everglades.

The term *boogery* comes from an old Welsh word, *bwg*, meaning "to scare." Eventually, the word was Anglicized into boo, bogus and booger. A hollow or holler is a narrow valley between hills and mountains. Of course, there is a **Booger Hollow** (Hall), or ghost valley, in Georgia. Now known as *Boozeville* (another type of haunt?), Booger Hollow was the site of early gold and diamond discoveries. Legends say that an eerie Boogeyman lurked in the hollers, but this was actually a tale circulated by local moonshiners in an attempt to keep the revenuers at a safe distance.

Bugaboo Island (Ware) is an island in the Okefenokee Swamp so named for tales of a frightened hunter who reported strange noises coming from the island. The "spook" was really noises caused by trees rubbing together in the wind. As a result, Bugaboo is sometimes called Spook Island.

Groaning Rock (Jackson) was the original name of the settlement. A nearby hollow rock formation produced a moaning sound when the wind passed over it. In 1904, the town's name changed to *Commerce*, site of multiple retail outlets (and, one presumes, less groaning of the pocketbook).

Ghost Hole Ford (Charlton) is said to be derived from a frontier killing involving a holdup and the shooting of a stagecoach driver. After nightfall, it became a haunted site where one could hear shots, screams and the wild thrashing of frightened horses. It's also said that the shooting may have been done by Seminole Indians, who were in the area until their removal in the 1830s.

Booger Bottom (Hall) is the site of an ancient Indian mound that now lies beneath the waters of Lake Lanier. Stories around Booger Bottom tell of a half dog / half cat hobgoblin that haunted the area. It was probably an invented spook again designed to keep away those nasty revenuers.

Enough about boogery. Time for fairy stories.

Fairyland (Walker) is the theme of Rock City Gardens and Mother Goose Storyland. Located on Lookout Mountain, **Rock City** is the main feature in this section. As the brochure reads, "Rock City is a true marvel of nature, featuring massive ancient rock formations, gardens with over 400 native plant species and breathtaking panoramic views from Lover's Leap, where one can see seven states from one spot." But it took an entrepreneur or two to see the possibilities of developing Rock City / Lookout Mountain into a tourist site.

During the Depression, clever entrepreneurs Frieda and Garnet Carter started developing a scenic garden location atop Lookout Mountain. Carved paths lined with indigenous plants led visitors to the scenic boulders and lookouts. Underground caverns with lighted fairy-tale scenes looked like the creations of magical creatures. The world's first miniature golf course was built there as part of the Carters' plan to develop a family/ tourist attraction known as Lookout Mountain and Fairyland Gardens. These would eventually draw thousands of visitors annually.

These were the days before interstate highways were lined with giant billboards designed to lure tourists to their designated spots. The Carters had an ingenious idea to paint barn rooftops along U.S. Highway 41, the route to Florida, or the "snow bird's" route. These signs, first painted seventy-eight years ago, urged tourists to "See Rock City," "See Beautiful Rock City, the 8TH Wonder of the World" or "Millions Have Seen Rock City. Have You?" Roof signs that read "Just 65 Miles to Rock City" let you know you were getting close. These painted barn roofs covered nineteen

"See Rock City today" painted atop a barn near White, Georgia. *Photo by Robert Gaare.*

states and were an effective, clever publicity stunt. Harley Warrick, who died in 1904, was one of the most famous Rock City barn painters. He was called a "Rooftop Rembrandt."

The barn signs once numbered nine hundred, but Lady Bird Johnson's Highway Beautification Act of the 1960s defined roadside signs as more of an eyesore than an icon. Signs had to be painted over. But a public outcry in favor of the painted barns led to a 1974 amendment to the legislation, calling these barn paintings "folk art." They were allowed to be repainted and remain.

Rock City itself maintains, frequently retouches and restores about one hundred of the original barns. Clark Byers and his son are hired by Rock City to do just this. Clark was struck by lightning once while painting a barn and said that was the end of his rooftop painting. Now, his son paints the barn roofs and Clark paints birdhouses with the Rock City advertisement on the roof. He used to paint mailboxes, too, until the U.S. Postal Service put a stop to that. His birdhouses can be found in many general stores.

13

MYSTERIOUS ISLANDS
OF THE OKEFENOKEE SWAMP

The mysterious **Okefenokee** (also spelled Okefinokee) Swamp area in Southeast Georgia occupies a great portion of Ware and Charlton Counties and parts of Brantley and Clinch Counties, covering some seven hundred square miles. The name *Okefenokee* came from the Creek Indians and means "trembling earth." Indeed, the earth in the swamp does seem to tremble, creating bubbling water and a series of floating islands, sometimes firm enough to hold one's weight. Freshwater marsh or mossy peat deposits spring from the tea-colored water and make it appear as if it's solid ground. One can step on it and won't break through, but the area will rise and sink for some twenty feet all around.

People no longer live in the swamp. Once home to Indians who were forced out in the 1800s, then home to Scotch-Irish "crackers" from North Carolina, the swamp then became the home of freed slaves. All were drawn to the area for its naval stores, turpentine industry, logging and bees. The mild climate and abundance of honey plants, such as the tupelo gum and the gall berry, attracted honey bees.

Of course, many legends and tall tales have sprung up about the floating islands of the swamps and the "Okefenokee folk" who once lived there. One whopper that still exists comes from Georgia's best-known traditional storyteller, Lem Griffis, who died in 1968. He often said, "See that honey a sittin' up there on the shelf? Well, I crossed my bees with lightnin' bugs so they could see how t'work at night, an' they make a double crop o'honey every year." Bees, alligators and bears all figure in swamp folklore.

Mirror image of cypress trees at the Okefenokee Swamp. *Library of Congress.*

Within the swamp are twenty-one nonfloating islands, large enough to be hospitable, including Billy's, Floyd's, Honey Bee, Jack's Wax, Scrub, Bugaboo, Mitchell's #1 and #2, Strange and Hog. It's time to talk about a few of them, how they got their names and the folklore surrounding the islands. It's been said that "a kinder or more hospitable people do not live." But that wasn't always true.

For periods, the swamp was a refuge for Indians avoiding removal, for escaped slaves and for deserters during the Civil War. Located at the northeast corner of the swamp, **Cowhouse Island** was given this name during the War Between the States because neighboring stockmen drove their cattle here to be spared from Union forces foraging on the land. Stories go back even before that, to the days of the Cherokee occupation. Indians purportedly herded their cattle here and also hid themselves from General John Floyd, of **Floyd's Island** fame, who was chasing them. It was also said that early settlers brought their cows to this island for the winter months, the land being fertile and the weather mild.

Billy's Island (Ware) was named for Billy Bowlegs, a leader of the Seminole who assumed leadership after the imprisonment and death of

Osceola, famed Seminole chief. During the Second and Third Seminole Wars of the early 1800s, a small party of Indians led by Billy Bowlegs evaded capture by retreating into the swamp.

The last Indian massacre in Georgia happened here. On July 22, 1838, Maximillan Wilde and his family of seven children spent a sleepless night worrying about a band of Seminoles who had been watching them. Why the Seminoles chose the Wilde family to attack has never been fully explained. Many of the family were killed, with only four of the boys and a neighbor's daughter surviving. Immediately, women and children residing in the area were sent to the safety of Fort Waycross while the men sought out the Seminole killers. There is no evidence that Billy Bowlegs knew of or planned the attack. It is reported that he was murdered in 1827, far in advance of said attack, but he was suspected, anyway. Actually, settlers and soldiers randomly referred to all Indians in the area as "Billy Bowlegs."

General John Floyd and his U.S. Army troops entered the area in October 1827, amassing on the southwestern section of the swamp. After a couple of skirmishes, Billy Bowlegs's Indians escaped the dragnet and fled south to the Florida Everglades. Billy Bowlegs's name became legendary, and the island was named for him.

The State of Georgia became the swamp's legal owner and authorized expeditions of surveyors and scientists to explore the islands. Others, like the Lee and Hebard families, saw the potential profits from such a piece of land, mainly in the harvesting of cypress and pine trees. Billy's Island flourished.

Then, in 1917, during the influenza epidemic, loggers thought that a good dose of whiskey would keep them from getting ill. The superintendent of the loggers found ten stills and ordered moonshine illegal on the island. Somehow or other, the logging operations continued, fairly wiping out the cypress population, until the U.S. government purchased the swamp in 1937. Modern conservation had begun, and a movement to preserve the swamp grew. President Franklin Delano Roosevelt inaugurated the Okefenokee National Wildlife Refuge, turning the area into a haven for tourists and wildlife.

Two of the most famous Okefenokee folk are known as the "King and the Queen of the Swamp."

King of the Swamp, Obediah Barber, stood six and a half feet tall. He was born in 1825 and was known for his strength, for his ability to tell a tale even while fiddlin' and for his three wives and twenty children. He lived on the north rim of the swamp for six decades and became a legendary

Photo of Obediah Barber's house in the Okefenokee Swamp. *Photo by the National Register of Historic Places.*

figure and symbol of the Okefenokee frontiersman. He was a fearless hunter, daring explorer and guide, a self-reliant swamp man renowned long after his death in 1909. His pioneer log cabin is a popular tourist spot in the swamp, being the oldest settler's cabin in the area and listed in the National Register of Historic Places. One surviving legend of Obediah is that he was so strong he could kill a bear with his bare hands.

Lydia Stone, born Lydia Smith and died Lydia Crews (for her second husband), was the Queen of the Okefenokee Swamp. She was almost as tall as Obediah, six foot, four inches, with broad shoulders and said to be extremely strong. Her father gave her a cow and a pig to start her on her way. Eventually, by buying and selling, she purchased her first forty acres of land, began turpentine interests and sold trees to the railroad for crossties. She bought land that timber companies had cleared and abandoned for mere pennies and died a millionaire. She was known to have said, "I always said I could make five dollars out of every one dollar I could get my hands on. I believe anybody can if they're careful and not afraid to work." Her home was in Racepond (featured in chapter 12).

14

TALES OF GEORGIA'S GOLDEN ISLES

Georgia's "Golden Isles" are a chain of barrier islands covering 150 miles of coastline, including Ossabaw, St. Catherine's, Sapelo, St. Simon's, Jekyll and Cumberland Islands. They were given the name *Golden Isles* by adventurers like de Soto and Pedro Menendez de Avilés, who were in search of gold. A different kind of gold was found there—one less tangible, but one that is more beautiful and longer lasting. Georgia's Golden Isles are composed of verdant, beautiful woods and sea marshes and are popular tourist spots.

First we turn the focus to **St. Mary's**, a river town, not a Golden Isle as such. St. Mary's is across the sound from Cumberland Island and named after the sixteenth-century Spanish mission of Santa Maria de Guadeloupe and the nearby St. Mary's River. Founded in 1787, it was the southernmost town in the United States when Florida belonged to Spain.

There are two legends of St. Mary's of interest, according to James T. Vocell's 1914 book, *Stories of St. Mary's: The History of Camden County.*

The first legend sounds vaguely similar to an Aesop's fable. A fair lady and early settler named Mary Jones found an aged chieftain named Withlacoochee sitting by a stream called the Sweetwater Branch. He had a thorn stuck in his foot. She removed the thorn. Full of gratitude, the old chief said that if she ever got into trouble, he would be there for her. A U.S. recruiting vessel began to solicit men to enlist in the navy around the time of the War of 1812, including her betrothed, Ben Johnson. She was heartbroken, thinking he would never return to her. Withlacoochee found her crying along the road. He remembered her goodness to him and his promise to help her. He took a handful of red berries and green leaves, scattered them on the waters of Sweetwater Branch and cast a spell. Whoever drank from these waters would return home safely. Her lover drank, as instructed, and returned home safely. This legend is still retold today.

Another story tells of St. Mary's in 1808, when it was a smuggling port for Spanish vessels. One day, a vessel laden with gin, rum and cigars dropped anchor in the St. Mary's River. Customs officers kept a sharp lookout, so the smugglers were unable to unload their goods. One dark night, the smugglers stole a horse from the local Presbyterian minister, carried it to his church and hoisted it into the belfry. The next morning, the entire population spent the day gawking at this sight and wondering just who the mischievous men were who put the poor horse up there. While suggestions went back and forth as to how to get the poor creature down, the smugglers unloaded their wares and were back out to sea unnoticed.

Sapelo Island, like many place-names in Georgia, is of Indian origin. It was called Zapala by Spanish missionaries and Sapeloe by English speakers.

We'll start with a brief history of Sapelo Island and then move on to the uniquely special **Hog Hammock** and the Geechee culture.

The island was privately owned for many years. Before the Revolutionary War, Patrick MacKay owned the island and then sold it to John McQueen, who sold it to a consortium of Frenchmen wishing to cultivate Sea Island cotton, cut live oak timber to sell to shipbuilders and stock the island with slaves and cattle.

Disagreements over the use of the island and expenditures led to the breakup of the partnership in 1705. It did not end well. One of the partners was shot to death by another partner in a duel. Another partner died of yellow fever.

The slavery ban was lifted in Georgia in 1750. Slaves proved to be a far more profitable source of labor to the colonists and their needs. The slaves brought with them knowledge of how to make tools for winnowing rice. Using the native sweetgrass found in abundance on the Georgia coast, they made sweetgrass baskets.

Sapelo was then acquired by three men, including Thomas Spalding, who purchased the entire island by 1843 except for a small tract of land called **Raccoon Bluff**. Spalding became a leading planter and agricultural innovator, introducing sugarcane to the state. He developed important techniques for the cultivating of Sea Island cotton, gradually developing

Sapelo into an antebellum plantation empire. He and his children owned more than 385 slaves.

No more famous slave arose from the Georgia Sapelo Island Plantation days than Bu Allah, sometimes spelled "Ben Alie," "Bul-Ali" or "Bilali." The Muslim headman of the Spalding Plantation, he was sold into slavery as a young boy. He could speak English, French and what was to become the Geechee dialect. The father of scores of children, he was beloved by the Spaldings and the slave community. Wildly intellectual and possessing an outstanding character, he had knowledge of herbal roots and secrets of the moon and tides. He wore a black cap, like a fez, and prized his Koran and prayer rug. After the slaves were freed, Bu Allah's children (he died in 1852) formed the First African Baptist Church, incorporating Muslim traditions into the Christian Church.

The Civil War ended the plantation economy. The Sea Island Circular, known as General William Tecumseh Sherman's Special Field Order 15, declared the barrier islands from Charleston and to the south to be set apart for the settlement of African Americans, freed by the Emancipation Proclamation and the end of the war. Whites were forbidden to enter the territory without proper authorization. Hopeful black homesteaders ran off the whites. Sapelo became the home to a large African American community during Reconstruction. A partnership of freedmen called the William Hillery Company, composed of John Grovenor and two other men, bought Raccoon Bluff. Over time, many of the former slaves purchased land on Sapelo, establishing permanent residences at **Hog Hammock**, Shell Hammock, Lumber Landing, Belle Marsh and Raccoon Bluff.

Sherman's orders didn't last long. Andrew Johnson, president after Lincoln's assassination, revoked them, restoring the land to the original owners. When the Spaldings returned after the Civil War, many former slaves left, especially with the looming threat of tenant farming hanging over them. They didn't see much difference between being a slave and being a tenant farmer. But Raccoon Bluff flourished and was fully owned by freed slaves. A community began to emerge with black people, free for the first time, making decisions for themselves. Those who stayed subsisted on what they could grow and on the local tidal food, and they built an oyster canning factory.

Eventually, the Spaldings didn't want to live there anymore. Their descendants sold most of their holdings to Detroit automotive engineer Howard E. Coffin. After twenty-two years, due to financial depression in the

The church at Hog Hammock, Sapelo Island. *Library of Congress.*

1930s, he sold the land to tobacco heir Richard J. Reynolds, who established the Sapelo Island Research Foundation. His widow sold Sapelo to the State of Georgia, the area becoming the Sapelo Island National Estuary and Research Reserve, a state and federal partnership.

When R.J. Reynolds took over the island, Raccoon Bluff stood in his way, as he wanted to create a saltwater marsh research foundation on the whole island, including their land. He offered to swap the residents their Raccoon Bluff land with houses in Hog Hammock that had plumbing and electricity. In spite of the temptation of modern accommodations, Hog Hammock was a less desirable area and had not been established in the way Raccoon Bluff was. Some residents refused to leave. Others moved on, mostly to the mainland.

Those who resettled in Hog Hammock cultivated gardens and built a schoolhouse. Hog Hammock became a 434-acre community that still exists on Sapelo Island. It was named for Sampson Hogg, an early resident, who was in charge of raising hogs for the Thomas Spalding family. Often, slaves were named for their occupation. The term *hammock* refers to a little island in the salt marsh, usually with red cedar, small live oaks and saltbush growing on it; it does not refer to the roped porch swing.

Hog Hammock's descendants were from the western "Rice Coast" of Africa. Slaves were brought from there to America to work on rice, cotton and indigo plantations. They spoke the Geechee dialect (usually associated with Georgia), as opposed to the Gullah dialect (usually associated with South Carolina). Both dialects are English-based Creole combined with languages from the west coast of Africa.

That brings us to griot Cornelia Bailey, who, along with the Georgia Sea Island singers, helped to maintain and protect the culture's unique heritage. Cornelia was a direct descendant of Bu Allah and author of the book *God, Dr. Buzzard, and the Bolito Man: A Saltwater Geechee Tale about Life on Sapelo Island, Georgia.* She was a member of the last generation of African Americans born and educated on Sapelo Island and became a vocal defender of Hog Hammock and its African American heritage.

For a period of her life, she lived on the mainland. In 1966, she returned to Sapelo to become the island's griot, the oral historian of their tribe, passing down the stories from thousands of years before. Her whole life was a struggle to fight the loss of her community's cultural heritage. She passed away in 2017.

R.J. Reynolds invited scientists to come and study the marsh. According to Bailey, "The change was a'comin'…when you explain something it goes away forever." She called Reynolds the "bukra," the kind of white man who gets in your business.

In 1950, Belle Marsh closed down. Lumber Landing ceased to exist in 1956, Shell Hammock in 1960. Raccoon Bluff closed down in 1964. All that was left was Hog Hammock. In 1967, electricity and indoor plumbing came to the island, long promised to the residents. In 1968, they built a new church.

Northeast Sapelo was sold to Georgia for a hunting and wildlife preserve. The Geechee people were being pushed off the island. A whole distinct culture of American life is in danger of being lost.

It is said that Hog Hammock is one of those places where visitors are welcome but invaders are not. As the population of the island dwindles, it's possible that the land will be sold to outside interests who have no love or concern for the unique history.

15

HO HO HO AND SILENT NIGHT

Georgia boasts two towns and place-names for both the secular and religious sides of our December 25 Christmas holiday.

Santa Claus (Toombs County), just past Lyons, was incorporated in 1941, with the first spelling being "Santa Clause." That was corrected (or modified) in 1970 to Santa Claus to attract more tourists to stop and take a look. Now the spirit of Christmas is celebrated year-round in Santa Claus, Georgia.

Driving on U.S. Highway 1, you are met with a cheery town sign. There's a statue of a very jolly Santa Claus / Saint Nick greeting you with the saying, "Welcome to Santa Claus, the city that loves children."

All the streets in the city are named with a Santa theme: Candy Cane Road, December Drive, Rudolph Way, Dancer and Prancer Streets, Noel Avenue and Sleigh Street. In the center of town is the post office with a mailbox out front. It's painted "Santa's mail" on the front and "Believe" on the side. Any Christmas card mailed at this post office in December is stamped with the genuine Santa Claus, Georgia postmark.

In Barrow County, on the way to Athens and the University of Georgia, is another Christmas town, **Bethlehem**, named for the city of David, birthplace of Christ.

The Bethlehem Methodist Church was established in 1796, but the town wasn't officially named and incorporated until some one hundred years later. Judson L. Moore (no known relation to Clement Moore of "'Twas the Night before Christmas" poem) was a well-known gospel songwriter and

The welcoming sign and statue in Santa Claus, Georgia. *Photo by Robert Gaare.*

The LED signage at Bethlehem. *Photo by Cathy Kaemmerlen.*

publisher who lived in the area. He suggested, "Why not name the whole town Bethlehem?" And so it was.

Bethlehem, Georgia, was dubbed the "Little Town Under the Star," with street names like Mary, Joseph, Judea, Star and Manger. A live nativity scene is staged annually. Each year, thousands of people take a pilgrimage to the Bethlehem Post Office to have their Christmas cards canceled with an old-fashioned postmark that reads "Bethlehem."

In 1967, a large group assembled in the town for the first day of issue of a Christmas stamp featuring the Madonna and child, based on a 1479 work by noted Dutch painter Hans Memling. A first-class postage stamp was five cents in 1967.

Although Bethlehem may be the little town under the stars, the LED town sign changes its message every thirty seconds, flashing such things as what day garbage pickup is and how many computers are available in the town library. It is a reminder that this is not the Bethlehem of yore.

There is a **Dasher** in Lowndes County, but it isn't named for the famous reindeer. The name comes from its first settler, O.P. Dasher, dashing any hopes of being a legitimate entry in this chapter.

16

FROM APPLES TO ONIONS AND POSSUMS TO BOARS

G eorgia citizens have long delighted in taking the name of a bird, animal, fruit or flower and turning it into an interesting place-name.

Crabapple (Fulton) is one of the oldest parts of Fulton County. First settled in 1874, the community took its name from a crabapple tree near the original townsite.

Ellijay (Gilmer) is "Georgia's Apple Capital." Ellijay comes from the Cherokee word for "green place" or "new ground." It's a fitting place-name for the green, red or golden apples grown here.

Tulip (Chattooga) is a ghost town, originally named for the yellow tulip poplar tree. In 1973, the town was reestablished as **Poetry**, Georgia. Resident Anne C. Otwell wanted to put "poetry" on the Georgia map and create a colony of poets. She was a fairly well-known Georgia poet, publisher of the *Poets Monthly Paper* and president of the Poets of Georgia Club. She was the mayor of Tulip before she renamed the town **Poetry**.

She and the town went broke; no poets moved there, and she lived as a hermit in the woods. When her "stomach started talking to her," she founded her own religious sect. She wrote her book *Bad News Gospel* and started the Church of Nudist Native and Naturalists with a Mission (NNNWM), changing her legal name to Serpentfoot.

She now lives in Rome, Georgia, and is considered an unorthodox Rome legend. She has been involved in many lawsuits, both for and against her. Her Rome history includes once disrobing in a county commission meeting as a protest. She has said, "I know what people say about me…that I'm crazy. I don't let it bother me. Some people just don't understand."

Her church is now called Our Greater Self Co-op. The message of the church is the need to preserve our greater self. In her own words: "That means we need to preserve our environment and nature in general. We are only a small part of this world in which we live, no greater or less than all the other animals and plants."

She frequently submits paperwork to have her name legally changed—again. Once, she requested her name consist of thirty-nine words that pretty much summed up her philosophy of life.

Now in her eighties, her time is no longer dominated by poetry but by good deeds. She frequently gives rides to those who have no transportation and helps prisoners and parolees who seek her help.

Her focus is to promote nature lovers and environmentalists. Her papers and works are part of the University of Georgia collection.

It's hard to follow the story of Tulip. **Flovilla** (Butts) is a coined name that means "village of flowers."

Vidalia (Toombs) comes from the contraction of *via-dahlia*, meaning "road of dahlias." But Vidalia is best known for its Vidalia onions, the official Georgia state **vegetable, grown** in a twenty-county region in **Southeast** Georgia. These trademarked onions are sweet, having more water content than the tear-producing variety of onion. Their sweetness has nothing to do with sugar content. No sulfur-based fertilizers are used, which helps lessen the pungency.

Moses Coleman, one of the first farmers to pioneer the Vidalia sweet onion, said he chomped on one in front of a Piggly Wiggly and had no tears, no grimace and no bad breath. **People were impressed! Piggly** Wiggly is headquartered in Vidalia and started to sell them—at first exclusively. Now they're sold everywhere. The Vidalia Onion Museum opened in 2011. It's not every day that an onion gets its own museum, nor can you go to the museum every day. It's closed on weekends.

Now we present some tidbits.

Persimmon (Rabun) is named for the wild persimmon trees growing in the area.

Sunsweet (Tuft) was so named for its bountiful sweet peach crop.

Sandfly (Chatham) was named by the early settlers for the persistently pesty sand fly.

Pavo (Brooks) comes from the Spanish word for turkey or the Latin word for peacock. This little town appears in Alan Jackson's video for his hit song "Little Man."

The Vidalia onion mascot at the Vidalia Onion Museum. *Photo by Robert Gaare.*

And so we've transitioned into towns named for animals. Perhaps the most famous is **Possum Snout** (Haralson), one of the early names for the town of **Tallapoosa**, an early gold-mining town. The name *Tallapoosa* is an Indian word of unknown derivation and also the name of a nearby river. The last two syllables of the name do sound similar to "possa" or "possum." Townspeople herald their former name, Possum Snout. The possum has been proclaimed the town mascot; his status celebrated each New Year's Eve with a possum drop.

Unlike the traditional possum drop of Brasstown, North Carolina, a real possum isn't dropped in Tallapoosa. It's a stuffed one, the work of local taxidermist Bud Jones. The story goes that Bud once spotted a dead possum on the side of the road while driving at night. Possums are often subject to becoming roadkill because of their nocturnal nature. Always looking for a new specimen to preserve, Bud noted that the possum was "not hurt at all, except he was dead." So he brought the creature back to his shop and wildlife museum to work on his new specimen. His possum "trophy" was put on display and named Spencer, after Ralph Spencer, a town founder who is given credit for the nineteenth-century boon to the town.

In the late 1900s, townspeople decided to create a New Year's Eve event inspired by Spencer and the town's early history as Possum Snout. Bud allowed the planners to use Spencer for the possum drop that would bring in the new year. The stuffed mascot is suspended in a wire ball wrapped in Christmas lights and kept at ground level so that spectators can have their picture taken with him. At about 11:30 p.m., he is hoisted to the top of the Cain Law Firm Building and at midnight is lowered to the ground amid a lot of hooting and hollering and cheering. This yearly event has caught the attention of local and national media and attracts a crowd two to three times the size of the community.

Gophertown or **Go'town** (Seminole) takes its name from the story of an enormous gopher tortoise, a burrowing land turtle and Georgia state reptile that was once killed there. The dried shell hung over the door of a community store.

Buckhead (Fulton) is now part of Atlanta. According to family lore, Henry Irby had a tavern and general store in the area in the 1830s where travelers, rich and poor, would stop for refreshments, supplies and gossip. As a talking piece, Irby once killed a buck deer and nailed its head to a tree near the store, where it remained for some time. Other legends attribute the placement of a "buck's head" on a post or tree to hunter John Whitley. Anyhow, the area became known as Buckhead. In 1998,

The Buckhead sculpture now located in front of the Buckhead Library, Atlanta. *Photo by Robert Gaare.*

as a tribute of sorts to the legend, Alabama sculptor Frank Fleming was commissioned to create his impression of the origination of the naming of Buckhead with a statue of a man with a buck's head surrounded by three brass dogs, three turtles and a rabbit. The statue is called *The Storyteller* and now adorns the front of the Buckhead Branch Library. He is surrounded by his woodland friends, but minus the turtles and the rabbit, who have gone missing.

There is also a **Buckhead** in Greene County with the same origin story. It's said that the natives in the area had an annual feast where they stuffed a buck's head with roots and placed various trinkets on the antlers. Then they mounted the decorated stag head in a high place facing the sun until spring.

Panthersville (Decatur) is so named from a legend of the Johnson family, who lived near Blue Creek. A son and his family came visiting one weekend. The son, returning to his home, encountered a panther appearing out of the wilderness. That panther must have made an indelible impression.

Roosterville (Heard) is a small community named by early resident Joe Spratlin, who said, upon hearing roosters crowing all the time, "Let's call the town Roosterville!"

Owltown (Union) doesn't boast of roosters crowing but of owls hooting—maybe for joy on hearing that the town was named for them.

GoatTown (Washington) isn't really a town but the name of a store and an intersection where goats sometimes escaped from the store and blocked the roads, much to the vexation of travelers in the area.

Rabbittown (Hall) is really a Gainesville, Georgia neighborhood, supposedly so named because rabbit hunters found an abundance of game here. An enterprising resident operated a commercial rabbitry in the area during World War II, when meat was scarce and rabbits were plentiful. A twenty-foot rabbit sculpture stands at the entrance of the strip shopping center, which includes the Rabbittown Café.

Some have said they were not impressed by Gainesville calling itself the "Poultry Capital of the World," erecting a big pillar with a chicken on top. So, not to be outdone, Rabbittown residents erected their own big pillar with the rabbit on top, which resembles a giant white-chocolate Easter bunny.

The café boasts good, old-fashioned, home-style cooking and is always crowded. Filled with rabbit décor, you can eat a full-sized meal for under ten dollars, the same price it's been for years. People love the place and come regularly or when they're in the area. "I have been eating here for over 25 years," writes one customer. And seniors get a discount!

Alapaha (Hamilton) is the blueberry capital of Georgia, even though the name *Alapaha* has nothing to do with the fruit. The name comes from a translated Creek word meaning "the other side" or another Indian word meaning "bear" or "bear lodge." It's also thought to mean "alligator." That's a lot of variety. Old-timers pronounced the town "Loppy-haw."

The giant rabbit sculpture in front of the Rabbittown Café. *Photo by Robert Gaare.*

The blueberries that give the town its fame are trademarked, like the Vidalia onion, and can be sold only by those licensed by the Georgia Seed Development Commission.

Alapaha made national news not for a blueberry or for Brian Buffington's song "The Alapaha Blues" ("the Catfish Dance"), but for Hogzilla.

Chris Griffin, a hunting guide, killed this twelve-foot-long wild hog, weighing in at one thousand pounds **and** nine-inch husks, on River Oak Plantation, a hunting and fishing site just outside of **Alapaha. It was** in June 2004. Was this a hoax, a myth or an exaggeration? There were two witnesses—Chris Griffin and Ken Holyoak, owner of the plantation, who took a photo of Chris standing in a pit beside the tied-up hog hanging from a tree. This, of course, was before burying him. **The photograph is** the only proof to the tale.

Holyoak said they didn't keep the meat because the meat of large feral hogs is usually not very good. The head of the beast was as big as a tire on a compact car and too heavy to hang on a wall, so they lifted him with a back hoe and buried him. Word spread. Local headlines read, "Town Eats Up! The Tale of Hogzilla" and "A Big Dig for a Big Pig."

That was that, until the Associated Press got **hold** of the story, and so did the National Geographic Society, which sent a team of scientists to exhume Hogzilla. They found a seven-and-a-half-foot carcass weighing around eight hundred pounds—still frighteningly large, but not record-breaking large. Chris and Ken had no scales around to weigh Hogzilla before burying **him**, so theirs was a guestimate.

There is a feral hog problem in Georgia. As noted in the story of Cherry Log, hogs in Georgia date back to the days of Columbus and de Soto, who brought the animals with them on their expeditions. The hogs spread into the interior and eventually into every county.

Feral hogs can also be domestic hogs that have escaped from farms. These animals can grow very large and become very mean. They don't need a reason to get mad and come after you. Feral hogs are omnivorous. A hog is always a pig, but not all pigs are hogs.

To further complicate this story, all wild pigs are known as boars. Feral domestic pigs start to take on the physical characteristics of wild boars after just one or two generations of being in the wild. The bottom line is that every one of these animals is just a pig. Those on the farm are domestic pigs, and those in the wild are wild pigs. But no matter what you call them, they make delicious pork chops and barbecue; that is, if they haven't grown too big, like Hogzilla.

The author wearing her "I Believe in Hogzilla" T-shirt. *Photo by Robert Gaare.*

Well, I'm a Hogzilla believer, and so are the residents of Alapaha, at least enough to have a festival in his honor with his own float at an annual community gala. Hogzilla put Alapaha, Georgia, on the map and turned Chris Griffin into a celebrity.

17

THREE EXPLORERS AND
A BUNCH OF BLOODY BATTLES

Three close-by Georgia "sister" towns are named for explorers
Christopher Columbus, Amerigo Vespucci and Hernando de Soto.

Columbus (Muscogee) was founded in 1828 and is considered to be
the last frontier town in the thirteen colonies, Georgia being the last
colony. The naming for Christopher Columbus was likely influenced by
the Washington Irving biography of the explorer, written in the same
year the city was founded. Irving was a writer of fiction and largely used
those storytelling skills in creating many of the myths surrounding the
explorer, including his discovery of America. This latter fact is not true.
Columbus thought he discovered another route to the East Indies and
not a new continent.

If anyone (other than the Vikings, for instance) should be given
credit for discovering North America, the honor should go to Amerigo
Vespucci, who indeed realized he wasn't sailing to the East Indies but
to the new worlds of North and South America. America was later
named for him, as was **Americus**. The name *Americus* is the masculine
version of "America." Three local men were appointed to select a site
for the Sumter County seat, which needed a name. There was such a
lively discussion about what the name should be that all who wanted a
chance to name the town put their suggestions on a piece of paper and
placed them in a hat. Isaac McCrary was the gentleman who pulled the
name "out of the hat": Americus, after the explorer. The Creek Indians
added to the name, saying it connoted safety from the elements of fury,

immunity to cyclones and floods. This turned out not to be the case, as the town was ravaged by an EF-3 tornado in March 2007.

The homespun version of the town's name comes from early leaders Wright Brady, Richard Salter, Jacob Cobb, Avery Wheeler and others who were so high-spirited as to be called "merry cusses," rowdy good-ol' boys. Each one individually was a merry cuss.

A local home-brewing association called itself the new version of the "Merry Cusses." Three of the local home brewers were photographed with President Jimmy Carter, who helped to legalize the home brewing of beer in the late 1970s during his presidential term. Although it was one of the minor accomplishments of his presidency, his action made an impact, helping to start the explosion of home brewing in the country.

Desoto, also in Sumter County, is so named from a story told of the explorer Hernando de Soto, who came through the area in 1538 and dug a well. Doesn't sound so impressive, but the story is interesting. Everywhere de Soto and his explorers went, there was violence and death to the native populations. The red and gold Spanish flag fluttered as de Soto's band of six hundred men came searching for gold.

They survived a bad passage through a swamp near Leesburg, crossed a small stream, then arrived in the future Desoto, exhausted and starving. They smelled the mouthwatering aroma of venison roasting on a spit over hot coals. El barbacoa greeted them, an early Georgia barbecue of wild turkey, deer and maize cakes cooked by a tribe of Creek Indians, who gladly shared with the explorers.

The hospitality was not returned, as the Spaniards mistreated the Indian maidens and seized supplies they would need to continue their journey. The Creeks retaliated by poisoning the drinking water. Exhausted, thirsty and unable to move on, de Soto and his men were forced to dig an artesian well that still flows freely in the area.

There was another, earlier Desoto in Floyd County, where the liquor ran freely. Its charter was eventually repealed, so the town name was up for grabs. Sumter County snatched it up. After all, de Soto and his men had their first barbecue there and dug a well. Now on private property and hidden, the well was a favorite picnic spot until 1920.

The Cherokees and the Creeks, despite de Soto and other explorers, managed to thrive and threaten the English and Spanish settlers on the border of Georgia and Florida. As a result, there were many bloody battles.

James Oglethorpe arrived in Georgia in 1733. One of the first of the "bloody" battles was at **Bloody Marsh** (Glynn) between the English and the Spanish, fighting over rights to the territory. Oglethorpe's troops watched the Spanish take protective cover (or so the Spanish thought) and began to cook their dinners. The British forces then opened fire, catching the Spanish troops off guard, killing about two hundred Spaniards and suffering few casualties themselves. The fighting was so intense that the marsh ran red with the blood of the Spaniards. Thus the area was named Bloody Marsh. Although Oglethorpe himself did not arrive until after the battle was over, he is credited with the victory.

Continuing to press the Spanish retreat to Florida, Oglethorpe used a trick. A Frenchman deserted from Oglethorpe's troops and joined the Spanish ranks. Oglethorpe made it look like the deserter was a spy. He sent a letter to the turncoat announcing his forces were strong and were about to get stronger with British reinforcements. This was a ruse. Oglethorpe knew the Frenchman would turn over the information to the Spanish. He did and was promptly executed for being a spy. Believing reinforcements were coming, the Spanish left the St. Simons area, ending their last invasion of colonial Georgia and securing Georgia as a British colony.

There are more "bloody" towns in Georgia, in fact too many to cover in this book. But here are a few more.

Bloody Branch (Charlton) was so named to commemorate an Indian massacre in 1794 of a settler named James Keene and his family. **Blood Mountain** (Union) was so named for a savage Indian war between the Cherokee and Creek Nations. It was said that blood ran down the mountain and colored the waters. **Blood Town** (Murray) was a Georgia frontier town where southbound cattle drivers penned their stocks at night for feeding and rest. There was no rest for the drivers, though, who purportedly reveled and brawled there, bloodying up the town from their fisticuffs.

Burnt Village (Troup) was a central point of the Muscogee, whose war chiefs met there to make plans for attacks on frontier white settlements. Many successful forays resulted. In 1793, several hundred warriors met here to celebrate their victories, dancing the Green Corn Dance. A Major Adams led his men to the village, seeking retaliation for the deaths of fellow settlers. Unaware of their presence, the Indians kept up their revelry until a late hour and went to sleep. You can guess what happened next. Nearly every warrior was killed, but the women and children were spared. The village was burned to the ground and was never again occupied by Indians. A few posts marked the site forever known as Burnt Village.

A painting of an Indian uprising on the Georgia coast. *Library of Congress.*

Torch Hill (Muscogee) is so named for the white settlers and their torches that were lit at night. They moved from place to place, lighting a torch here and there, to confuse the Creeks as to their location. Eventually, a major battle ensued, wiping out the Indians.

Hornet's Nest (Elbert) was the name given to an area where a number of Patriot Whigs lived. They were vindictive, like mad hornets whose nest has been invaded, in their hatred of the Tories and the Redcoats. Nancy Hart, Revolutionary War heroine, lived in this area. There are many tales told of her outsmarting British soldiers in the area.

Once she saw a Patriot and a neighbor running for his life, being chased by a band of Tories. Nancy let down the bars in the fence around her house, allowing the man to ride his horse through her house and out the back door. She put up the bars again, shut her doors and tied a rag around her head, pretending to be sick. When the Tories arrived, they demanded to know if she had seen that "Patriot devil." She asked, "Why are you disturbing a poor, sick widow woman?" They left, going the wrong way in pursuit of the Patriot.

The most famous story concerning Hart is when a band of Tories came to her house and demanded she cook them dinner. She obliged, wining and dining them. Then she took advantage of their gluttony and drunkenness by sneaking their guns—one at a time—out a chink in her log cabin wall and into the hands of her waiting daughter, Sukey. When

143

Print of Revolutionary War heroine Nancy Hart, holding the redcoats at bay. *Library of Congress.*

a soldier discovered what she was doing, she quickly picked up his gun and killed him (according to some versions of the story). She then killed another soldier who advanced toward her. When her husband returned with a band of Patriots, they hanged the remaining British soldiers. Their skeletons have been recently unearthed, adding validity to this tale. (See more about Nancy Hart in chapter 1.)

Mad as a hornet? Indeed! Beware if you're wearing a red coat. Today, the *Hornet's Nest* is a quarterly publication by the Georgia Sons of the American Revolution.

18

SPRINGS, SPAS, RESORTS AND SIGHS

Georgia has its share of springs, healing waters and resorts known for their restorative powers. They continue to be popular tourist sites. Some of the main ones are included here, as well as the folklore and details behind their names.

Jay Bird Springs (Dodge), the town, was named after a local spring. Supposedly, the waters of the spring healed the injured leg of a man who was led to the place by a jaybird. Georgia's first public swimming pool was built here, utilizing the waters of the natural spring that came from the adjacent Gum Swamp (not so appealing a name!). Jay Bird Springs is now a spiritually based rehabilitation center.

White Sulphur Springs (Hall) was discovered in the early 1800s by two hunters who tracked a deer, came upon the spring and drank from it. All of their ailments were immediately healed! I'm not sure about the absolute truth of that last statement, but the springs contained sulfur, which was valuable as a medicinal liquid. The name is self-descriptive. The springs later became a busy place for families and visitors who came to regain their health or to escape malaria fever during the summer months.

Indian Springs (Butts) is a town that originated with the Creek Indians. It was so was named after the nearby creek where the natives collected the water for its healing qualities. It was called the "Saratoga Springs of the South," with many seasonal tourists coming to the springs for the curative and homeopathic power of the sulfur water. The pressure of underground forces brings water to the surface, picking up many minerals during the process and causing the sulfur smells.

The most famous watering hole in the area was at Indian Springs. It's thought to be the oldest state park in the nation, acquired from the Creek Indians in 1825 with the Treaty of Indian Springs. Chief William McIntosh was killed by the Creeks for signing this treaty, considered to be a treasonous act to the Creek Nation.

Mineral Springs (Pickens) was known in the late 1800s and early 1900s as a place to go to for relief from many ailments, including gout and migraines. I'm wondering if each spring at one time catered to different ailments.

Warm Springs (Meriwether) is perhaps Georgia's most famous spring, being the site of Franklin Delano Roosevelt's Little White House. The spring waters here are naturally warm, heated by the inner earth in a pocket of rocks some 3,800 feet deep. With the water being eighty-seven degrees year-round, the springs served as a natural therapeutic center for victims of polio, like President Roosevelt. In fact, he began the Warm Springs Foundation, which operated as a therapy center for polio victims and those suffering from other crippling diseases. The Little White House, where President Roosevelt died on April 12, 1945, from a massive cerebral hemorrhage at the age of sixty-three, draws more than 100,000 visitors each year.

Sandy Springs (Fulton) was once a rural village and summer retreat on the Chattahoochee River. Now it is the seventh-largest city in the state. Sandy Springs originated as a watering stop for Native Americans who frequented its bubbling springs. It quickly became a community in the 1800s as settlers moved into the area. Today, the original "sandy springs" can be found at Heritage Green, a four-acre city park that is operated by Heritage Sandy Springs, a nonprofit organization dedicated to the history and culture of the community.

Cave Springs (Floyd) is located in Rotater Park, just outside of Rome. Legend has it that tribal meetings and games of the Cherokee were once held there. The natural limestone cave and springs are the namesakes of the town. The small cave has impressive stalagmites and a pathway leading to the

Franklin Delano Roosevelt swimming in the warm waters of Warm Springs. *Photo courtesy of the Roosevelt Museum.*

The author drinking from the pure water at Cave Springs. *Photo by Robert Gaare.*

Devils Stool Formation. It looks like a throne for someone or something from the underworld. The spring water has won awards for its purity and taste and is commercially bottled. People come here with empty jugs to be filled at the spring, to take home the delicious, pure drinking water.

During the Atlanta campaign of the Civil War, both Confederate and Union troops came to Cave Springs for hospitalization and rest. Of interest is nearby **Chubbtown**, founded as a colony of free blacks in 1864 by Henry Chubb and named after him. Another exception to the inclusion of a town named after a man, Chubbtown was spared destruction by the Union army.

Radium Springs (Dougherty) is best known as one of the Seven Natural Wonders of Georgia and is the largest natural spring in the state. Known previously as *Blue Springs*, the deep blue waters empty into the Flint River. The springs were called Sky Water by the Creeks, who traveled for miles to bathe in the waters for the curative powers. Native Americans believed this place to be nothing short of magical. Warring tribes converged at the springs for talks. Only peace could be discussed in this magical place. They tried to keep these springs a secret from the Spanish explorers looking for the fountain of youth and so used tricks to guide them far away.

The water contains trace amounts of radium, thought to be healthful at the time. The discovery of the mysterious radium became a gimmick for the springs to attract tourists. Taking advantage of the obvious draw, Blue Springs was renamed Radium Springs. Radium water was thought to be an elixir of youth, banishing all manner of disease, from anemia to high blood pressure and from gout to arthritis. Providing the basis for a huge quack-medicine industry, these fanciful notions about radium and radioactivity would not be dispelled for decades. Several deaths were attributed to radium poisoning, but not at Radium Springs.

As it turned out, there is not enough radium in the Radium Spring waters to be dangerous, but the springs are incredibly radioactive, causing the waters to glow a faint luminescent blue. Bottling the water and selling it as radon water turned out to be a fluke. Its half-life was just 3.82 days; by the time the bottle reached the customer, most of the radiation was gone.

In its heyday, you could slide or dive from the high board into the bowl of azure blue water and then get warm on the sandy beach. Indians believed the body of blue water led to the spirit underworld. The depths of the pool were unknown for a long time. There is an extensive underwater cavern system in the area.

In 1920, a casino and entertainment center, complete with a glittering ballroom, were built overlooking the sapphire blue springs. Although the casino never offered gambling—illegal in the state of Georgia—it became a popular spa and resort. Northerners stopped by on their way to winter in Florida to swim in the springs. Its heyday was in the 1960s.

A fire in 1928 destroyed most of the building. It was rebuilt to its former grandeur, only to be severely damaged by the flood of 1994 caused by tropical storm Alberto. It was called the flood of the century, a once-every-five-hundred-years flood. In 1998, the area was again flooded, this time by the "son of the flood of the century" that damaged the buildings beyond repair. FEMA ordered the building torn down in 2003, and Radium Springs has been closed ever since.

Nothing has been rebuilt. FEMA has labeled it a flood zone. To be rebuilt, preservationists would need to move the building above the flood zone, taking away from the beautiful view of the springs. The Georgia Department of Natural Resources purchased forty-five acres of land nearby to preserve the springs themselves. It is now a habitat for Gulf-striped bass and for botanical gardens, walkways and kiosks. Swimming is no longer allowed. Radium Springs is one of several "blue holes" along the Flint River's bottom.

Travelers Rest (Stephens, Macon and Pike) is the name for several stagecoach rest stops in early Georgia history. The Travelers Rest in Stephens County is the most famous, an eighteenth- and nineteenth-century tavern and stagecoach inn designated a National Historic Landmark and now a state-run historic site. One of the oldest inns in Georgia, it was erected by Major Jesse Dalton, a Revolutionary War soldier and Indian fighter. He built it to accommodate adventurers on what was called America's "western frontier."

In the late 1700s, Northeast Georgia was Indian country, and only the bravest ventured into the "frontier." The frontier was land to the west, past Augusta. Indian uprisings continued well into the late 1700s. In 1815, the Unicoi Turnpike was completed. Within a year, this highway became a major north–south route. In 1819, the entire route was ceded by the Cherokees to the State of Georgia. It was no longer considered the frontier, especially after the Cherokees and Creeks were forced to leave the state, and travelers began to venture out more extensively. They would need places to rest and to eat. Travelers Rest and others served that purpose.

An English guest once wrote about the inn: "Here I got an excellent breakfast of coffee, ham, chicken, good bread, butter, honey, and plenty of good new milk for a quarter of a dollar. And a clean, comfortable place to stay for the same price!"

Travelers Rest was later called Jarrett Manor when it was purchased by Deveraux Jarrett, the richest man in the area. Three generations of Jarretts inhabited this plantation, purchased by the State of Georgia in 1955. Today, visitors can tour the house and see many original artifacts and furnishings created by Caleb Shaw, a renowned cabinetmaker from Massachusetts.

There is also a stagecoach stop named **Travelers Rest** in Macon County, later incorporated as *Bristol*. Another **Travelers Rest** was in Pike County and later was called **Jolly**. (See more in chapter 9.)

19

A BIT OF WHIMSY! A BIT OF OOPS!

The place-names in this section are sheer fun and mostly based on folklore. Some are whimsical. Some are desperation names. Most are good for a laugh and a head scratch.

Jot-Em-Down (Pierce) is not so much the name of a town but the name of the general store, which in some cases was the entire town and was located at a major crossroad. Jot-Em-Down was a common name for a weed-and-seed general store. The name derived from the store owner "jotting down" what the customer purchased and allowing him or her, on credit, to pay later. There is an unincorporated community called **Jot-Em-Down Store** in Pierce County, Georgia. **Doctortown** (featured in chapter 4) had a store called Smith's Jot-Em-Down.

Po Biddy Crossroad (Talbot) sits at the junction of Po Biddy Road and U.S .Highway 80. The story goes that a mother hen had a brood of little biddies. One of them ran into the road and was killed by a horse. Someone exclaimed, "Well, that's the end of that po' biddy!" But it was the beginning of the town. Others say the name originated over a chicken dinner, with one guest taking the last piece. Another guest then remarked, "Well, there goes the last of the po' biddy." And that's the last of that story.

A newspaper clipping reported that the citizens of **Rough and Ready** (Clayton) were "rough and always ready to fight," as they did in the Civil War, when Confederate general William J. Hardee had his headquarters at the Rough and Ready Tavern. His plans were to set up his troops in a position to fend off the Yankees, preventing them from taking control of the railroad line south of Atlanta.

But there is another possibility to the name's origin. There was a tavern here that was a stagecoach stop on the line from Macon to North Georgia, later to become the first railroad station south of Atlanta. It was said the passengers were "rough" from the ride and "ready" for a good meal.

When a troop of show people from a long time ago paused in a small haven to ask for directions to a village where they could perform, a resident suggested, "Why not do it here?" A large, gaudily dressed woman and a performer in the show asked sarcastically, "What town?" The resident glanced at the woman's once-beautiful, fancy silk dress, now the worse for wear, and replied with a chuckle, "Split silk!" And **Split Silk** (Walton) became the name of the town.

Nahunta (Brantley) was originally a freight station called Victoria. There are many versions of how the town came to be called Nahunta. One version is that the town was named for an Iroquoian word thought to mean "tall trees." Another version claims the city was named by a turpentine producer who came from Nahunta, North Carolina. Another story relates that so much freight was consigned to a timber operator named N.A. Hunter that the railroad men called the town N.A. Hunter's Siding. The name was shortened to Nahunta. A final theory, on the racist side, states that Indians came here from the Okefenokee Swamp. They spoke English poorly and would grunt, "No hunter," for the name of the town.

Shakerag (Fulton) has a number of tales of its place-name derivation. One is that the name was based on the slang word *scram*. Communities named Shakerag were made up of residents who were tough and ready to take on any stranger who didn't belong. He was chased away by a resident, shirttail out, who was shaking his rag (his shirt) and sending the stranger a'-scramming.

Once there was a tavern at the corner of McGuiness and Bell Ferry Roads in Fulton County. A fight broke out. The lady who ran the tavern was so upset that she told the fighters to "shake your rag outside and don't fight inside this tavern!"

Another local legend says the name was given to the settlement by train engineers, who could see the laundry hanging out to dry on the tree branches, bushes and fences. They would see the washerwomen shaking out their rags. Mondays were popular washdays, and clothes could be seen "shaking in the wind."

Others say the name refers to the waving of a signal flag at early railroad stops.

Still others say "shaking out your rag" refers to shaking out the gold dust collected when panning for gold, gold being found in this area in the early 1800s.

There are at least half a dozen Shakerag communities in Georgia.

Deep Step (Washington) was the name that postmaster Gus Avant submitted to the U.S. Post Office Department (USPO). He took the name from the nearby Deepstep Creek banks. They were steep and had to be crossed downstream, where it was less steep and less deep. Local legend explains that a man accidentally put his foot down in a large hole here and exclaimed, "Ugh. Deep step."

Snapfinger (DeKalb) was the name of a town and a creek where a surveyor tripped and broke his finger. Because he "snapped" his finger, the name Snapfinger was applied to the area.

Snapping Shoals (Newton) was named for an old Indian fishery where the fish could be pitched out or "snapped" as they passed over the shallow shoals.

Boxankle (Monroe) is now called Richland and is in Stewart County. It was said that once, some men were watching a cockfight. Two men argued over the results of the match. One knocked the other over a wooden box and broke his ankle. Thus the community was called Boxankle.

Lord a Mercy Cove (Union-White County border) is a deep and steep, sloped valley and part of the Appalachian Trail. This whimsical name may have come about when travelers first saw how steep it was and said, "Lord a mercy," wondering how they would ever make it down.

Metter (Candler) residents have a saying "Everything's better in Metter." It's a laid-back town known for saying, "If we have a fire on Saturday, we put it out on Monday." Perhaps the town is laid back because of the Guido Gardens, a quiet place to pray, meditate and ponder.

There are several stories about how the town's name came about. Some say the real name suggested for the town was mistaken by the USPO. Both *Metter* and *Leonard* were submitted. The official who made the decision thought that Metter must be the name of a good-looking local lady, so he chose that name. But Metter was not a lady's name but a made-up name by Dr. Dan Kennedy. Or was it? Some say the town was named by a railroad engineer who said he met her—his wife—here, so he named the town Metter.

Resaca (Gordon) was named by soldiers returning from the Mexican War, desiring to honor their great victory at Resaca de la Palma, meaning "dry bed of the palm." But a much more interesting legend, funnier to men more than women, relates to a young Indian brave who was to select a bride from several who were brought before him with sacks over their heads. After making a choice, the sack was removed, revealing her face. After seeing what his choice looked like, he commanded, "Re-sack her," thus the name *Resaca*.

Another USPO mistake is attributed to the naming of **Fort Valley** (Peach). The townspeople applied for the name *Fox Valley*, but it was misread or there was a typo, and the name came back as *Fort Valley*. There has never been a fort anywhere around this town, but the name stayed.

Stillmore (Emanuel) had a similar USPO goof. A list of names was suggested by the USPO, but none were acceptable to the townsfolk, who asked if still more names could be sent. Apparently not, as the townspeople gave up and used the name Stillmore.

A similar story involves the naming of **Nameless** (Laurens). After submitting several hundred names to the USPO authorities, none was found satisfactory, so the townspeople gave up and called their town Nameless.

Hopeulikit (Bulloch) also submitted many names to the USPO for approval. All were rejected as already being used, so the townspeople, out of desperation, submitted the name Hopeulikit. Apparently the USPO did, for the name stuck.

Box Springs (Talbot) was named for the boxes railroad agents placed into nearby springs in order to collect water for the passing steam engines. It was first called Box Spring, but townspeople permanently added an "s" after saying the name incorrectly for years.

In addition to some of the place-names already listed, quite a few more towns obtained their names because of an "oops" moment.

Needmore (Brantley) came about when customers criticized the local general store for not having enough supplies to choose from. They cried out, "We need more!" And the name stuck.

Reka (Bryan) is a shortened form of *Eureka*, so named because that term had already been taken.

Chatsworth (Murray) was so named because a sign fell off a freight car on which was printed the name Chatsworth. The sign was picked up, placed on a pole by the tracks and became the basis for the town's name. Of course, others say the town was named for a railroad official named Chatsworth.

The name **Dashboard** (Carroll) truly came from an "oops" moment, when Slick Chamber's mule kicked the dashboard of Cecil Spruell's new buggy and caused some damage. The mule dashed away and was no more—at least, not that I can find. But the name of the town stayed.

Gum Pond (Mitchell) came about because the residents couldn't spell the name *Cypress Pond*, the name they preferred. But they could spell Gum Pond, and that name stuck.

Wrens (Jefferson) was probably named for W.J. Wren, who obtained the land in exchange for two blind horses. It's the boyhood home of Erskine Caldwell, who wrote *Tobacco Road* and *God's Little Acre*, observing the life of a sharecropper and describing it as "no more obscene than life"—or exchanging land for two blind horses.

Kite (Johnson) was named for Shaderick Kight, who donated the land to build the town. He chose to simplify the name in order for it to be easily spelled and to facilitate rail service to the town.

Dip (Hall) was the former name of *Clermont*. Harvey Ruth, the first postmaster, decided on this short, simple name because he had no cancellation stamp and had to do the cancellations by hand. Dip was chosen because it was short and easy to spell. The name might also refer to the town's location, a dip between the mountains and ridges.

Nankipooh (Muscogee) got its name from the Gilbert and Sullivan opera *The Mikado*, written in 1885. Nanki-Poo was the son of the Mikado. But this can't be correct, because the town was there long before 1885. The Biggers family, which played a prominent part in settling Nankipooh, said that the name was that of a great chief of the Muscogee Indians, who were there before the white settlers arrived. The Indians left the area on the Trail of Tears in the 1830s. So, this is more likely the name's source. The local newspaper, the *Nankipooh Enquirer*, uses the subtitle "Covers the South like Sorghum Syrup," with no reference to the opera.

Poster advertising Gilbert and Sullivan's operetta *The Mikado. Library of Congress.*

No doubt a favorite Georgia place-name is **Enigma** (Berrien), whose naming was an enigma, so the name stuck. According to Bernice McCullar, nobody nearby knows where the name came from or why. John A. Ball, an early settler, said he found it "a puzzle to name the town," so Enigma's naming will forever be an enigma.

The following place-names are just fun to say and need no comment: *Boozeville, Boneville, Butts* and *Bogart*.

So that's the end of that.

ABOUT THE AUTHOR

Cathy Kaemmerlen is a professional actress, storyteller, playwright, author and historical interpreter known for her variety of one-woman shows and characters. Through her own production company, Tattlingtales Productions, she created and currently performs, along with other actors she employs, over thirty in-school curricular-designed programs with a social studies and language arts emphasis. A recent honor was performing her one-woman show about Rosalynn Carter for the former First Lady and President Carter three times, the last performance being at the Rylander Theatre in Americus, Georgia. A Hambidge fellow for over twenty years (where she writes many of her shows and books), she has now written five published books, including three through The History Press/ Arcadia Publishing.

She's a lover of stories and collects them wherever she can find them. Her own state of Georgia, the "Peanut Capital of the World," has proven to be a treasure trove, resulting in books like this one about Georgia place-names.

She lives in Kennesaw, Georgia, with her husband, Robert Gaare, and two cats, Bitsy and Betsy, who are best friends. She is the mother of three wonderful children and has three granddaughters, who are her greatest delight. Check her out at www.tattlingtales.com or www. cathykaemmerlen.com.

For more stories about her travels while researching this book, you can check out her journal on her new author website, www.cathykaemmerlen.com, or find out about her other books.

Visit us at
www.historypress.com